THE RELATIONSHIP DANCE
Moving to Deeper Personal Connections

D1521654

LINDA RAY CENTER

TRD-4

ISBN: 978-0-9979202-7-7

Email: lindasondancer@gmail.com

http://www.therelationshipdance.com/

DEDICATION

To the One who I trust to direct my steps and who will not let me fall; dancing with Him, I couldn't help but follow.

And to my Mother, Claire Ray; she is my partner in unconditional love.

ACKNOWLEDGEMENT

Thanks to my family and friends who allowed me to share their stories. Connections with you have provided my happiest days.

This book would not be possible without my editor, Joyce Farrell; your revisions astonish me.

Love to my husband, Bill, for your feedback and support.

A heartfelt thank you to my loyal friends: Eglaide Seiber, Ann Kling, Nancy Hood, Joy Sterling, Celeste Gill, and Cathy Burkhead for the shared vision. Without you, I would have missed the dance.

CONTENTS

THE RELATIONSHIP DANCE
Moving to Deeper Personal Connections

PART ONE

Dance With Me

For decades, I dreamed of the perfect spouse, the ideal family, and flawless friendships, but there is nothing perfect in ourselves or relationships. People can't measure up to our expectations, nor can we measure up to our own. The journey has left me tired, frustrated, and lonely, but also hopeful. Humans never stop yearning for connections that touch us both physically and emotionally.

I mess up often, but I find God's wisdom in Proverbs 4:26: "Mark out a straight path for your feet; stay on the safe path." That verse provides the clearest way for me to handle relationships. I've also discovered His lessons never cease.

In the Bible, Jesus shows an obsessive love for people. The Samaritan woman at the well in John 4 was an outcast. Although, speaking to her was forbidden, Jesus defied the culture customs and said to this woman, "Give me a drink." His request wasn't about a cup of water, but a way to get closer to her.

Each person who enters my life brings challenges, and I have been able to meet those challenges by discovering a personal connection with God and not relying on my feelings. His love for me is the best instruction manual in knowing how to love others. Part one of this book will show how God presents Himself and His perfect love. Part Two will explore how friends, neighbors, co-workers, and family members have approached God on their journeys.

The Lord has been faithful to put people in my life who have more experience in writing than I do, and who can help me communicate what has shaped my heart. From past experiences, I knew if I struggled in serving God, I was doing my will, not His. He sends strength in a scripture found in Psalm 27:14: "Wait patiently for the Lord. Be brave and courageous." Achieving the best balance between stillness and busyness is not easy; being peaceful and taking action both can help me to glorify God if I allow Him to show me the correct balance. Waiting is hard, but there are a lot of rewards in learning patience.

This past year has been a lesson in endurance as I struggled with deciding what to write and determining how to express my passion. Persistence paid off because uncovering ugliness, whether orally or on paper, brings healing. The Bible says to confess your sins to the Lord and to admit your mistakes to each other. Not long ago, I overheard a minister say, "Your mess can become your message." Some might categorize mistakes as wrong choices, but what needs to be examined are areas that can keep you stuck or rob you of enjoying people.

I'm eager to share how God joined my friends and loved ones to dance in unity despite our differences.

Let Our Feelings Go

Understanding is the key to help us get through.
Wisdom from the Bible has some valuable clues.
Relationships can change as they move to and fro,
That leads to confusion that's out of our control.

People aren't perfect, and it's easy to proclaim,
I wasn't in the wrong and will not take the blame.
Each day brings challenges to maintain unity,
It's sad to live in a conflicted community.

Judging others will destroy harmony within.
Then before you know it, arguments will begin.
Each opinion might be different, but let peace flow.
Show love for each other and let our feelings go.

Life Isn't a Dress Rehearsal

One July morning as I got dressed to go to the beach, I wondered which hat I should wear. It wasn't really about the hat; it was about the role. As far back as I can remember, I was always playing a character. My hats transform me from a plain Jane to a flashy Felicia.

When I was ten my sister, Andrea, was born in Albemarle, North Carolina. When baby Andrea arrived, I knew I had to fly out of the family nest to make room for her. There were many hours to figure out how to entertain myself while my mother took care of the baby. When most little girls were playing with baby dolls, I pretended to be a proprietor of a country store in the screened back porch of my parents' house. There was excitement in pretending somebody might drop by, and I could sell them something.

After a few weeks, my mom wanted me to take the store apart and clean up my mess. Daddy thought my store had been a cute idea, and he told me I had a gift of being a person in charge, but acquiesced to my mother saying, "Mind your mother, and get rid of the shop."

Much later, I realized that being independent and ambitious at an early age would follow me into adulthood. My top priority was to make things happen and to carry out my goals. My Dad called me his "goal-obsessed princess."

Dad was always busy looking for the silver lining of life, but he was chained to the world. He was living without peace, joy, or purpose. We moved around a lot. Dad was always looking for that perfect job, a bigger house, a better neighbor, and something exciting to do or buy. While he was trying to find the perfect situation, his family was pulled along with him.

It was a challenge to attend six new schools in twelve years and scary too. Moving around forced me to be self-sufficient. You learn fast to be tough or be gone.

One good thing about moving around was I looked forward to being able to take dance classes in different studios. Several of my dance instructors told me to find my unique personal style and not be a carbon copy of one of your teachers. That would be easy since I didn't stay in one place long enough to copy anyone's style. As frustrating as it was moving from one location to another, I was developing my individual flair. The summer of 1960 I was ten years old and my parents moved to Brandon, Florida. I tried to make friends with the other kids in the neighborhood, but it wasn't easy. My parents moved so often that it seemed like I was always the new kid trying to fit in.

School started a few weeks later, and I overheard some classmates talking about camp and how they met new friends. As I walked down the main hall to my classroom a poster on the bulletin board caught my eye. I stopped to read it: *Memorize a thousand Bible verses and go to a Bible camp free*. I remembered the conversation I overheard a few weeks earlier and thought to myself, *That's it! I can do that, and afterwards I'll make friends*. Do you know how hard it is for a ten year old to memorize one thousand Bible verses? It took three months of waking up early and getting to school thirty minutes before the bell rang. Then I had to recite three to five verses to the teacher. I would watch the teacher check off the verses—-ten, twenty, one hundred, five hundred— until one day I had hit the one thousand mark quota.

The next summer, I found myself sitting on a bench waiting for supper at a Baptist Bible camp. A teenage counselor joined me and said, "Hi! I'm Rose. Are you having fun?"

I replied, "Yes. I can't wait until tomorrow."

"Why is that? By the way, what is your name?"

"My name is Linda, and I'm excited about tomorrow because it's horseback riding day."

"So you love horses?" she asked.

Before I could answer she said, "I love Jesus, and did you know He loves you?"

"Yes, I know the song, *Jesus Loves Me*," I said.

Rose took a small Bible out of her backpack and put it on her lap. She took a deep breath and asked, "Do you know you're a sinner?"

"A sinner! I'm only ten years old how could I possibly be a sinner? I don't smoke, drink or cuss."

She grinned and said, "Let me show you a verse." She opened the little book to Romans 3:23 and asked me to read it out loud.

I read, "For all have sinned and fall short of the glory of God. "

All of a sudden my heart started beating faster, and it was hard to swallow.

She repeated, "Jesus loves you, Linda," then went on to say, "God sent His Son to suffer and die on a cross just for you. Then three days later, He rose from the dead so you can be adopted into the family of God."

In an uncertain tone, I asked, "He did that for me?" I started fidgeting because there was a knot in my stomach, and I knew I was going to cry.

Rose pulled out a tissue from her backpack and asked, "Do you believe me, Linda?"

I whispered, "Yes."

Rose stayed and prayed with me. I didn't understand completely, but that evening changed me as I accepted Christ as my personal Savior.

The next day, Rose came looking for me. She said, "I forgot to tell you, there is a verse in the Bible, II Corinthians 5:17 that says, "*If anyone is in Christ, they are a new creation. Old things are passed away*." I have to run and make a staff meeting. See you later. "

I stood there dumbfounded watching her run to the office. I didn't look different, but felt overwhelmed by happiness. I had a new friend that would be with me always and His name was Jesus. I couldn't wait to go home and tell my mom and dad what had happened.

I had a happy childhood and watched Mom every morning exercise to the Jack LaLanne television program. I developed my love for movement and dance during her exercise time. She was a stay-at-home mom, and Dad was the breadwinner. He made her account for every penny she spent. My dad allowed me to take dance classes after much pleading from Mom and me. I remember my dance instructor asked if I wanted to dance a solo. She explained the routine would cost extra and when I asked my father, he said, "No, we can't afford it." I ran to Mom for help. She came up with a plan; we spent hours walking the back roads of Brandon to find Coke bottles, then we returned the bottles to the store for five cents each. Good ol' Mom figured out a way for me to have a solo performance that last year in Florida.

When I was twelve, my family moved to Calvert City, Kentucky. Instead of fearing another move, I decided to take part in my dad's race for adventure. After a few months in our new home, I started my first business teaching children in the neighborhood how to dance. I taught the classes at my house on the covered concrete carport.

The cost of each lesson was twenty-five cents, and the children in the class thought that was a deal since they could use my old dance shoes and were provided a costume for the recital. I loved the adrenalin rush when I was making up dances, teaching, performing, and, most importantly, being in charge. That was the beginning of being chained to power and position. I spent my time thinking how I was going to be successful and make a lot of money when I was an adult.

Tumbling into my teenage years, I found myself moody and thinking more about boys than God. Also, I attended three high schools before I graduated which caused me to become very independent and self-sufficient. I stopped going to church because I felt I didn't need God's influence any more. I was taught as a youngster to stand on my own two feet. I didn't need anything from anybody, not even God.

The next move, when I was fifteen, landed us in Terre Haute, Indiana, for two years. It was a nightmare trying to fit in. I got along fairly well with the boys, which made the girls hate me. The last week in school I had a solo part as a 1960's mod go-go dancer in the year-end musical. I was eager to show off my moves in white knee-high boots, a red fringed dress, and my new flip hair style. I began my routine in a cage with a lighted sign on top and with my name in lights. On opening night, I arrived at the school theater, and a group of four girls tore my costume, dismantled the cage, and broke the sign into pieces. I was horrified, but I finished my performance with the attitude that the show must go on. I was determined not to give up.

After Terre Haute, we pulled up stakes and moved to Milan, Tennessee, where I finished my senior year of high school in 1968.

After I graduated, I wanted to attend college and major in dance. When I asked my dad to help me financially, he told me

I needed to work my way through college like he did. Although, he would not help me with money, he would help find me a job. His answer and attitude didn't set well with me.

I was angry at my dad, so instead of college or a job, I got married to a baseball jock and lived in Jackson, Tennessee. The marriage lasted for three years.

Unfolding Relationships: John

John was in his third year of college, and I married him right after my high school graduation. Looking back, I did this as an excuse to get out of my parents' house. After twenty-five years of marriage, my father had asked Mother for a divorce. I couldn't stand the confusion and arguing. Besides, I was ready to conquer the world.

After my husband graduated from college, he tried out for the Seattle Pilots. The Pilots were a professional baseball team based in Seattle, Washington, for one year; they later moved to Milwaukee and became the present-day Brewers. The wives weren't invited to the training camp, so I didn't have a choice but to go back home and wait until his training was over.

John got cut from the team six weeks later, after the first season, and we returned to everyday married life in Jackson, Tennessee, where he had gone to college. I got a weekend job as a dance teacher for a big studio in Jackson, and during the week, I had a fulltime position as a sales clerk in a department store to make ends meet. John was looking for a job. I noticed he spent a lot of time away from home, and when he was home, he didn't have a lot to say. We were rarely intimate, and John was always irritable.

After several months, John came home early one evening. I can still remember what he said. "Do you want the good news or the bad news first?"

"The good news," I replied.

"I found a big-wheel job in the city today." I watched his expression change as he continued, "Since I have come home from Seattle, I see you in a new way."

"What way is that?" I asked.

"You're an average-looking girl with a high school education and couldn't possibly help me advance myself in life. I want a divorce."

With a shaking voice, I said, "You can't be serious."

He started walking to the bedroom saying, "I am."

I stood there frozen and thought, *What next?* Then I heard the closet in the bedroom slam shut. I ran looking for the noise and found my husband pulling out the suitcases. He said, "I'm leaving."

"Oh no you're not! I'm leaving!" I screamed.

I ran out the door to clear my head, or maybe in the hope that he would run after me.

Forty minutes later, I returned to an empty house.

After the divorce two months later, I found I was driven to succeed. *How dare he think he was superior to me? I'll show him.*

I had one goal in my mind, and that was to succeed. I was a woman on the run, pushing anybody out of the way to get to the top. I thought I could accomplish anything on my own and knew how to make it happen. I was waltzing down life's road called *the Free Will Freeway*.

I looked for work in the performing arts field that would support me. Through friends, I heard about a movie being filmed in Jackson called "Walking Tall" that was hiring locals as extras. I jumped at the chance to make the money and to get the experience. Little did I know how being in that movie would become part of a giant leap into a successful dance career for over thirty years!

When the movie was finished filming in 1971, my parents called me. They said they missed me and wanted me to move where they lived in Dalton, Georgia. I didn't think I had anything to lose, so I drove the six hours to Dalton. My dad surprised me by setting up a dance registration at a local high school on the next Saturday morning. With my father nudging me, I registered two hundred students that day, and my dancing career started off with a bang. I called Dad after registration to tell him how many students signed up. He said, "I guess the ad I put in the paper announcing you as a cast member of "Walking Tall" did the trick."

"Daddy, you're brilliant!" I exclaimed.

"Always remember, Princess, you have to have a gimmick."

I found a modest apartment in an unsafe part of town, but it was all I could afford. My parents helped me move in. When Dad left he said, "You need a few dead bolt locks. I have an extra set and will come early in the morning to install it."

Two days after classes begun, I was still asleep one morning when I heard a knock on my apartment door. I shot straight up in bed, wondering if it could be Dad at this hour. I turned on the small table lamp, and reached for my watch. It was 4:35 a.m. I walked down the stairs, tying my robe, and I yelled, "Who's there?"

"It's your mother. Open the door." I noticed my sister standing there first looking dazed. Then my mom's cool demeanor caught my attention. She was in shock as she said, "Get dressed and come with me. Your dad died this morning."

I shook my head in denial as I tried to throw some clothes on. Stumbling to the car where my mother and sister waited, I wanted answers. In a shaky, disbelieving voice I asked, "How?" Then, "Why?"

My dad had died of a massive heart attack. It was instantaneous, and he didn't suffer. My mother had heard a loud thump and found him on the kitchen floor. The refrigerator door was still open as if he was reaching for something to drink. My mom couldn't find his pulse and called

911. The medics and ambulance arrived quickly to take my dad away. My mom rode with them. The doctor on staff at the hospital pronounced him dead.

After the funeral, I threw myself into my business. For five years, I rented different commercial buildings to use for my studios, but finally I thought it was time to buy a piece of land, build a structure, and make payments on something I would own one day.

I used every spare moment to look for land. I found the perfect building site and inquired about a commercial loan. Once the loan was approved, I hired some workers. In a few weeks, the building crew started construction. The building took about three months to erect. It consisted of an office, a waiting room, the main studio, two smaller studios, and three bathrooms.

I hired and trained extra staff to accommodate all the newly-enrolled students. Besides managing the business and teaching class, I found myself spending a lot of time ordering dance shoes, leotards, tights, costumes, and accessories for my customers, so I turned one of the smaller studios into a dancewear shop called Dance N Things.

The enrollment had skyrocketed, and the dancewear store was doing extremely well. If I needed a hat to celebrate success, it would have to have been extra-large for my big, prideful head.

A few years later the number of students outgrew the studio's space. The academy offered acrobatics and dance, but the class most in demand was gymnastics, especially during Olympic years when parents dreamt of Olympic medals for their daughters. I started looking to expand my existing studio, or, alternately, to find another commercial lot close by on which to build a gymnastic facility. It was easy for me to get ideas, figure out ways to implement them, and then to gloat with pride at my abilities. If I set my mind to any goal, I was sure I could make it happen!

Coach

In the middle 80's I took a few dance students to a Dance Master convention in Atlanta one weekend where I met Coach Lane. He was a guest instructor teaching a back handspring class. Coach was a college professor in Georgia and had made a name for himself as an Olympic trainer. After the class, I made a point to talk to him and invited him to come to Dalton for a workshop for my gymnastics students.

After the workshop, I found myself calling him for advice and flirting with him, even though he was married. After a few weeks, he asked me to be his traveling instructor for the dance aspect of the competitive floor exercises he coached.

We spent a lot of time together, and one thing led to another. Before I knew it, he was getting a divorce and asked me to marry him. We didn't marry for love; we both married for business purposes. He told me he was tired of being on the road making other gymnastic schools successful and wanted to have a home base where he could develop his gym. I had the perfect location for a gym and had done the groundwork. It was easy for Coach to take over and expand the program. I was proud of his credentials and expertise and knew those would increase enrollment. All in all, we married for the wrong reasons.

Two years after we married, I decided to add on to the studio. I contacted the doctor who owned the land directly between his office building and my facility and asked if he would be interested in selling the lot between us. The doctor's words rang in my ears. "Sorry, Linda. I am keeping that lot to sell to a professional person." When he said that, I had an intense desire for revenge. I slammed the phone down and thought to myself, *I'll show him who's professional*!

A few weeks later I inquired about the property on the other side of my building. The land contained a church—the Happy Valley Baptist Church. The building was old, but the property was prime—a corner lot on a major street across from Dalton High School. It didn't take long to get my loan approved by the bank. It took Coach and me approximately nine months to tear down the church and erect a pre-engineered, metal building. Coach Lane wanted to invest his retirement money in a fully-equipped gymnastic facility, and I couldn't have been more pleased with the idea. At first, Coach spent a tremendous amount of time and effort on our businesses, but, after the new building was in use, I found I was spending more time at the gym and office than he was. I started to be dissatisfied in my marriage, mostly because I was the partner who was more dedicated and driven. When the pressure from traveling to run clinics, teaching at the gym, or taking care of paperwork became too much, he would regroup by going to his second home in south Georgia. I would be left taking care of the business alone, making me even more resentful.

After eight years of seldom seeing eye-to-eye about the business, one Friday afternoon I walked to the gym to see if my husband was ready to teach class. To my surprise the door was locked and there was a note on the gym door: *Closed.*

I ran back to the dance studio and called him screaming, "What is going on with you? Your classes start in one hour!"

He replied, "You're too demanding. I need a break from you and the business. We don't have a marriage; it's more like a business contract. There's more to life than working twenty-four hours a day, seven days a week."

Gasping for breath, I asked, "What am I going to do about your classes?"

He exclaimed, "You figure it out!"

I don't remember what was said or done to get through that day, but I knew one thing—I had to survive.

On Saturday morning I called Bert, my on-call handy man to change the locks. Next, I called my attorney. While his phone was ringing I knew what I was going to do wasn't fair, but then business sometimes isn't fair.

On Monday morning, I was in the studio when my husband knocked on the door, "My key won't fit. Let me in!" he demanded.

I snapped through the locked door, "No! You don't belong here. You're not responsible, and I don't need you anymore. I filed for divorce. Go back to where you came from."

Standing with my back against the door, I didn't dare move. I hoped he would fade out of my life and that I would have the business all to myself. I got my wish; Coach didn't fight back. He just walked away. In the following weeks, I was excited about the new possibilities of running the business myself.

The academy was extremely successful. I worked virtually twenty-fours a day teaching, cleaning, ordering workout apparel, attending gym competitions, or holding birthday parties and sleepovers on the weekends. I didn't own a business; the business owned me.

We enrolled over three hundred students most years, and during Olympic years there were close to four hundred. Our students competed in dance and gymnastics and received many awards. Everyone in town wanted to attend classes and there was a waiting list of potential students. Pride flooded my thoughts with, *Look what I have done; see what all I have accomplished.* I used Coach, depleting his retirement funds to help build the gym I wanted and then confiscating most of his gymnastic equipment. I took every opportunity that came my way to step up on the success ladder. No matter what I achieved, it got harder for me to be satisfied at each step.

After my divorce from Coach, I found myself jumping from one relationship to another. I enjoyed the experiences and had the mindset there would always be another partner available. Taking risks is what I grew to love. My thinking set me up for unhealthy lifestyle patterns. Later, when I married my fourth husband, Lee, it was another new risk.

A Story of Abuse: Lee

While waiting to purchase stamps at a local post office, I overheard that a bar named Crazy Cowboys in Chattanooga, Tennessee, was offering free country line dances every Sunday afternoon. In 1992 country line dancing was the biggest dance trend, and everyone in my hometown, wanted to participate.

I returned to the dance studio I owned, where I ran into Holly, one of my dance instructors, and asked her if she would go with me to Crazy Cowboys to take a few dance lessons. She enthusiastically replied, "Yippee! That sounds like fun!"

Driving to the club, I said to Holly, "After we learn the dances, we can teach them at the studio."

She snickered and said, "Miss Linda, you're always finding new ways to make a dollar."

We arrived at Crazy Cowboys and found our spots on the dance floor. A few dances later I needed to take a breather and write down some dance notes. Finding a quiet corner, I opened my dance bag, pulled out paper and pen, and started to jot down the combinations. When I looked up, I noticed a dark-haired, handsome man staring at me. He had a young boy around eight beside him, and they were talking. The guy walked up to me and introduced himself as Lee. He winked and exclaimed, "You look good on the dance floor." I took that as a compliment. We introduced ourselves to each other, and Lee handed me his business card. I could see that he owned a real estate brokerage.

Minutes later, the boy joined us and asked, "Dad, can we go? I'm bored."

"Just a second. This lovely lady's name is Linda." Then he turned his gaze to the left and said, "This is my son, Raymond."

Since I didn't see a wedding ring on Lee's left hand, I inquired, "Is this your weekend with Raymond?"

Rolling his eyes, he replied, "Is it obvious?"

The three of us were making small talk when Holly approached. She squeezed my arm and said, "I'm ready to go."

I grabbed my bag and jacket. As Holly and I were leaving, I heard someone call my name. I turned around to see Lee pantomiming, "Call me."

The next morning as I got ready for work, I noticed Lee's business card on my nightstand. I picked it up, and could smell a hint of his cologne. Nervously, I dialed his number. Hearing his voice sparked the memory of how appealing he had looked the day before with his sexy dark green eyes and alluring smile. We chatted a while, and I was careful not to give out any information about me, my children, or business. Before we hung up, we agreed to meet at the Steak and Ale restaurant in Chattanooga the next Friday.

At the restaurant, Lee was waiting for me in the lounge with a drink in his hand. He helped me with my coat and the foul smell of alcohol on his breath made me wonder how many drinks he had consumed before I arrived. He was the consummate charmer, he pulled out my chair and urged, "Order anything your little heart desires."

After we decided on our food and he order it I started our conversation with, "I really like your cologne, what it is?"

Stroking his jaw bone he replied, "Its Polo."

"Do you like to read?"

"Not really."

"What do you do for fun?"

He laughed, "Pick up pretty ladies at country-western bars."

I looked him straight in the eyes and asked, "You're not a murderer are you?"

The evening flew by, but we had little in common, and he was five years younger than I was. Nevertheless, I told myself all of that didn't matter, because across the table was a gorgeous hunk of a man. We enjoyed our dinner then afterwards Lee escorted me to my car. He opened the door for me, I got in, and then he leaned over. For a second I thought he was going to kiss me good night; instead he reached for the car seatbelt to snap it closed. "There," he said, "You're safe to go home now."

Monday at work, I received a bouquet of roses with a note that read, "Friday night was incredible. Are you available this weekend?"

Later in the evening, Lee called me at home to see if I had received the flowers. Before we hung up, we made plans for Saturday morning.

We met at a coffee shop in Ringgold, Georgia because it was half way between his condo and my house. Lee told me he liked to gamble and enjoyed fishing with Raymond, and he told me about a few women he had been involved with. After a few hours of consuming coffee, he asked, "I know where a great pool room is. Let's head that way, shoot a few games, and have a pitcher of beer."

I didn't want a beer at 10:30 in the morning, much less a pitcher. "I need to go back to the gym and oversee a birthday party at noon," I explained.

Sipping a drink of water I noticed there was a frown on Lee's forehead, and he said rudely, "Really?"

As I observed his body language and heard the tone of his voice, my gut feeling told me to take the time to know this man better.

We continued to date every weekend, and Lee kept pushing to meet my family, visit my workplace, and see my house. Eventually, I gave in because, simply, he was irresistible.

Our weekend dating turned into every other night. I liked all the attention but felt smothered. When I had my doubts, he would turn up the charm another notch. Soon after, he announced he was moving to Dalton so he could be closer to me.

By the time we had been together for three months, he became possessive of my friends, time, and whereabouts. I was concerned, and felt similar to a fly caught in a spider web. Lee made a plan to capture me, and I couldn't get out. I was an adrenaline junkie and addicted to him and the rush he provided. He introduced me to fast cars, gambling, and partying—things I had never experienced before. In the past I had spent my days and nights at my business, doing my best to provide financially for myself and my family. Lee's bad-boy ways thrilled me to the core. With him, I could let go of responsibility, let down my hair, and let someone else be in control. I couldn't get enough of him, like an electric current seeking an outlet. A few months later it didn't surprise me that he wanted me all to himself and insisted on getting married. With the hairs standing up on the back of my neck from either caution or excitement, I said, "Yes."

One evening, close to our wedding day, we went to a party. After a few drinks, Lee got upset when he saw me talking to one of his friends. I could see his eyes across the dim-lit room following my every move. Lee had folded his arms across his chest and stomped his way toward me. He poked his finger at my chest, put his mouth close to my face, and said, "You're flirting." Then he grabbed my arm in front of everybody, and snarled, "We're leaving!" Everyone in the room became silent. "Now!" he growled and pulled me outside.

I struggled to get free from him all the way to the car saying, "I can't believe what you just did."

Then he pulled the car door open and pushed me into the car. I was too scared to move. He took the wheel and started down the highway. He was driving like a wild man, reaching speeds in the nineties. The tires squealed as he turned onto my street. The car came to an abrupt stop in front of my house. Still shaken by what had happened at the party and the thoughts of a crash, I didn't try to get out of the car. Instead, I sat perfectly still, sobbing. I cried so hard my eyes were stinging, and my mind was in a state of shock. I came back to reality when Lee opened the door and jerked me out of the car. He pulled my engagement ring off my finger and threw it across the yard. I had never seen that side of him before. I tried to calm him, but he was too angry. When he went to get his cigarettes out of the car, I ran to the front door, unlocked it, and yelled at him to go home. I ducked inside, shut the door quickly, and leaned up against it. My heart sank; I knew the rage was about something much more deeply immersed than the fact that I was talking to his friend.

That night should have been a big red flag, but I chose not to see it. In a way, I felt I deserved his anger. I tried to detach myself from Lee because I knew this relationship was going nowhere but on a destructive emotional course, but I failed, in part, due to my low self-esteem.

Lee called twenty times a day until I finally decided to answer the phone. I knew he would try to smooth-talk his way back into my life, and he did. I made excuses for Lee's behavior; for example, his ex-wife had full custody of their son, and she was upset that he was getting married again. She refused to let Raymond see Lee, and I knew that was bothering him. As before, I repressed my emotions and went forward with the wedding hoping he would fill more secure after we got married. Since Lee worked most weekends, we planned a short honeymoon to Nashville.

After four days in Music City, we were returning home when Lee stopped at a convenience store to buy a pack of cigarettes. I remained in the car and noticed another car pulling up beside ours. The driver glanced over, and we locked eyes for a second as he got out of his car. I assumed he had looked my way to see if he recognized me.

After a few seconds, Lee came rushing to the car, opened the door, sat down, and threw his arms up in the air and said, "I saw everything and how you were enjoying that man looking at you." I thought, *Not again!*

"Let me explain," I started.

He cut me off by snarling, "You're nothing but a piece of trash."

I took a deep breath and pleaded, "I'm completely committed to you and have no interest in another man."

Mumbling under his breath, he pulled the car onto the highway. I knew better than to say anything in my defense as it would just aggravate the situation.

Lee's verbal abuse continued until we got home. We unpacked our bags, made small talk and got ready for bed. Before I turned off the light Lee said, "Linda, I love you and don't want to lose you. I will work at being more secure in our relationship."

I nervously replied, "As far as I'm concerned, your outrage and stupid jealousy ruined our honeymoon." I pulled the covers over my head, turned over and thought about asking

God if I had made a big mistake. I feel asleep with that thought lingering.

The next morning, I had some time to myself before going to work. I sat in my favorite chair with the lights off, trying to figure out my relationship addiction with my husband. I had been so wrapped up in the emotional merry-go-round with Lee, I had ignored God, and, in the dark, I wondered what God would say about my marriage.

I walked on eggshells trying hard to keep Lee's anger in control and started to relax for a few months.

On a Sunday evening in the spring, I was coming home from a dance convention. As I drove up my driveway, there was enough light to see my clothes were thrown all over the yard. There was a pile of glass at the front door, and the garbage can was full of shoes. I ran into the house and saw Lee was drunk and looked mad. I was baffled and shouted, "Why is all my stuff outside, and where did all the glass come from?"

He grabbed my hand and pushed me to the kitchen, and I noticed the glass top on my dining table was missing.

Lee put his hand on the side of my face and shoved it toward a piece of paper lying on the counter.

His fingers wrapped in my hair and forced my head down, barely missing the corner of the upper cabinet. He snapped, "It's my tax return. Do you see how much I owe this year because of you? I pay you half of the house expenses, but you get all the deductions. When I came home from the accountant, I lost it. I took a hammer and busted up your table. After that, I went upstairs to your bedroom, and decided you needed to suffer a bit too, so I threw your clothes and some of your shoes outside to show you I'm the head of this house."

I started laughing hysterically and yelling, "I wish I had never set eyes on you, more less married you. I want out."

"You want out? I'll be happy to oblige."

He dragged me out the back door, and locked it behind me. When I banged on the door, he turned the lights out one by one. I banged and banged figuring Lee was sleeping it off. My handbag with my money and identification was inside, it was late, and I didn't know what to do. Helpless, I spent the night outside on the steps with the door as my pillow.

The next morning, I was awakened by the door opening and Lee standing there looking ragged and hung over. He said, "Tell me what happened last night; I can't remember much."

I told him everything including that I wanted a divorce and didn't want to live in fear any more. He pleaded, "Please, please, give me another chance. I'll do anything you ask. I'm begging you."

He acted so sincere, and I could imagine his pain. I said, "On one condition—you go to anger management classes and seek help. Meanwhile, I'm going to a friend's house for a few days."

"Okay, okay, I promise to find a program today."

For three weeks in a row, he went to classes. He called me every day, sent flowers, and brought me something to eat at the studio between classes. Since he was working on his problem, I decided to come back home.

Things were quiet for a few days, and I decided it was safe for me to be home. After a month, things were getting better and I thought the anger classes were helping him. One night I returned home late from teaching a dance class. Lee had been home fixing us something to eat and as soon as I walked inside, he started accusing me.

"I know you weren't at the studio all this time, where were you?" He tore the sleeve off my leotard, then he started shaking me yelling, "You slut! Who have you been with?"

He released me and grabbed his car keys off the counter, He said, "I'm so sorry. I'm going to take a drive and cool off."

He left, and I was relieved he didn't hurt me physically this time.

I was finishing eating dinner when I heard him drive up. I didn't make eye contact when he entered the kitchen. I filled his dinner plate and was walking to place it on the kitchen bar when Lee grabbed the plate from me and threw it across the room. Food and broken china were everywhere. In disbelief, I grabbed a dish towel and started cleaning the walls and floor. Lee put his hand on my back to stop me. I froze. He lifted me up and started saying he was trying, but the thought of me being with another man drove him insane. We sat up all night and talked.

"I want to tell you what I did after our last fight. I was in such despair, I bought a gun."

"Why would you do that?" I asked.

"I thought everybody would be better off if I were dead."

I sighed at first and though it was only a scare tactic. "Go on."

"I stopped going to the anger classes last week and thought we should get marriage counseling instead."

I have never been around domestic violence, but I knew enough to know I was a victim of it. I started my quest to understand all I could about abuse and codependency. I secretly called a domestic violence hotline to get as much information as I could.

The hotline's advice to me was to think safety first, and counseling was a good idea. We had been married a little over two years when I found a marriage counselor. She came highly recommended, and after a month, her recommendation was to get a divorce. She said, "Linda's a bird and needs to fly. Lee is a fish and must have water to survive. Even though the fish and bird love each other, the bird can't survive in water, and the fish can't fly."

We walked out of her office speechless and stood outside the building to process what she just told us. I felt relieved that a professional saw the potential danger in our relationship, and I thought she was right about our marriage being unfixable.

Lee was furious and said, "That brainless counselor doesn't know anything. You probably set her up. Our wedding wasn't a mistake, and divorce isn't an option." My legs felt like bags of rocks were tied to them as I shuffled my way back to the car.

After we got home, I felt like I was back in a prison cell and needed time to plan my escape. However, once again, Lee's winning ways overpowered my thinking, and he convinced me to stay.

A month later, we went to Biloxi, Mississippi. Lee was quite good at blackjack and anything connected to gambling, and he wanted to go to a casino there. I was hoping for a fun weekend without any fighting. After several hours, watching him gamble and drink, I decided I had enough and needed to get some sleep. I told Lee, "I'm going to our room."

He kissed me and said, "I'll be up shortly."

When I woke up the next morning, I found Lee had never come to bed. I dressed and went back to the casino to look for him. I found him at the same blackjack table where I had left him the previous night. I walked up to him and said, "I have been looking for you. You never came to bed. Are you okay?"

"I lost all my money," Lee said. Then he sneered, "Do you have any?"

I said a firm, "No."

"I'm tired then. Let's go home." He yawned and asked, "Will you drive?"

As I drove, I occasionally glanced at him, sound asleep in the passenger seat. My gut feeling told me he would take out his losses on me when he woke.

We arrived home, and I left him in the car hoping he wouldn't wake up too soon. I went inside and immediately called my girlfriend, Joan.

"Joan, I have to talk fast before Lee sees me using the phone," I whispered.

"Is everything okay? I mean, are you all right?"

I said, "Lee acted strangely this weekend. I will explain later, but I'm scared. Can you be on standby in case I need you?"

The next moment, I heard the door bang open, and I hung up the phone quickly. I scrambled for the shower and turned the water on. I heard footsteps bounding toward me. Lee kicked the bathroom door open and before I could speak, he pulled me from the shower, leaving red welts on my arms. While I struggled to get my balance, Lee pushed me hard to the floor and I tasted blood. He opened a drawer, grabbed a pair of scissors, and pressed them into the back of my neck. His lips came close to my ear as he spoke intensely, "If I can't have you, no one will." I was terrified and screamed for him to release me. Seconds later, I felt the sting of a cut, and I fell to the floor. Lee walked out of the room. I laid there curled up and motionless, hoping to regain strength. I tried to remember the last time I prayed, but, I couldn't. As a result, I offered God a crisis prayer asking Him to help me. I had been a believer since the age of ten, but somehow had drifted away from God. Under my circumstances, I had an urgent need to find my way back to the Father. I trusted Him to show me how to survive.

I used the counter to pull myself off the floor. Then I made an attempt to clean myself. I reached for a hand mirror to check the back of my neck and saw that the scissor tips barely broke the surface of the skin. I put some ointment on the cut and crawled into bed feeling every sore muscle in my body.

Suddenly, I heard Lee approaching the bedroom, I quickly pulled the covers over my head and pretended to be asleep. He laid on top of the covers with his clothes and shoes on and immediately passed out. As I listened to him breathing, I knew I must leave him the next morning.

As soon as he left the house, I gathered up a few personal belongings and called Joan to ask if I could hide at her house. My friend was relieved when I knocked on her door later. She took pictures of the scratches on my face, my black eye, a broken front tooth, and the scissor cut on my neck. I contacted an attorney and made an appointment that day, so I could put a restraining order on Lee and begin divorce proceedings.

The second thing I did was call the dentist. I wanted to know if he could save my tooth that was chipped when Lee pulled me out of the shower, and my mouth hit the floor. I made an emergency appointment later that day.

Friends and family supported me in my decision to divorce Lee, and I was grateful to God for helping me out of my situation. However, I soon began to loosen up and felt my need for God beginning to fade.

After the papers had been served, I heard he was dating Raymond's mother. I returned to my home, buried myself in work, and attending church every now and then, trying to put the past behind me.

On a Saturday morning two months after the divorce was final, I received a phone call.

"Hi. Linda here."

"This is Lee, how have you been doing, Girl?"

In a cold tone, I responded, "What do you want?"

"My son left a few items in the house. Since I'm off today, I would like to pick them up."

I almost spouted *Okay* when I remembered the abuse hotline told me think safety first, so I suggested we meet at a Waffle House on Interstate 75 at the Ringgold exit.

"All right, all right," he said.

I said anxiously, "I'll meet you in one hour."

I had packed Raymond's books and games a few weeks ago, so I grabbed the bag, changed my clothes, and headed to Ringgold.

I found Lee sitting in a back booth in the coffee shop, a waitress came over and asked, "Do you want to look at a menu?"

"No, just a glass of water," I said.

Meeting Lee's glaze, my intuition told me our get-together was a mistake. He looked terrible. He was much thinner, and his pupils were dilated with dark shadows under his eyes. His skin tone was different, and he reeked of cigarette smoke. Lee's hands were twitching as he reached for mine across the table. His cleared his throat and said, "We need to talk. I've missed you. You must come back to me."

I jerked my hand back and said, "No, I'm not. This meeting was a set-up, and I'm leaving."

At that moment he knew he wasn't in control—I was—and he banged his fist on the table to get my attention. "I will get even with you."

Sliding out of the booth, Lee took the glass and threw the water in my face. I glanced at the waitress coming to my rescue with a towel but didn't wait around. I rushed for my car and didn't realize Lee had followed me until I looked into the rearview mirror to back out. He threw something at the vehicle and yelled, "Get out of the car, damn you! I said, *Get out of the car!*"

I somehow maneuvered my way out of the parking lot and drove straight to the interstate.

God's presence surrounded me as I drove home, and I felt His Spirit was sending warning signals. Pulling into my driveway, I paused to push the garage opener, and the same warnings kept spinning in my head. I decided to react, and so I backed out of the driveway, and headed for my dance studio. There, I called the police and asked for help entering my house. I described the scene with Lee at the restaurant, and I explained about the restraining order. I told them I felt he wanted to harm me and my property.

I waited at the studio for a few minutes to give the police time to arrive at my house, and then I drove home with a single thought—no one should live in fear of another person. The police were waiting as they watched me enter the garage. When I opened the car door, I could smell the nauseating scent of Polo cologne. Entering the kitchen, I noticed some items were out of order, and a cigarette butt was smashed into the floor. While the police were searching upstairs, the phone rang. I looked at the caller ID and sighed. I reached for the phone and quivered, "Hello."

Breathing hard, Lee said, "I'm calling from a phone booth ten miles away. I can't take any more. I have nothing to live for without you."

I thought about the night he told me about buying a gun, and I still thought he was bluffing. I heard him crying uncontrollably saying, "Linda, I don't want to die." He hesitated and repeated, "I don't want to die."

I didn't know how to help myself, much less him. I thought that this was only a new trick to suck me back into his dark world. I remained silent with tears running down my cheek and fear running up my spine.

Lee interrupted the silence with, "Promise me…"

He never finished his sentence. I heard his phone drop and hit the side of the booth. Then I heard the sound of a door opening, and, finally, running footsteps that grew softer and softer.

The police found me sitting on the floor by the phone, propped up by the wall with my legs pulled up under me. They stayed for a while to make sure Lee wasn't coming back. Before they left, they told me to lock the doors behind them and to call if Lee returned.

Later, I was too afraid to fall asleep, so I sat up in bed with a kitchen knife beside me in case I needed it to protect myself. The sound of the grandfather clock intensified with each gong of the chimes. The dripping of the faucet drove me crazy, and the wind outside never quit howling.

Several hours had passed when lights appeared in the driveway. I glanced at the clock; it was 3:00 a.m. I had kept the phone next to me and started dialing 911 when the lights suddenly disappeared. I dropped the phone and darted to the window to see Lee's car pulling away. I thanked God for standing between me and evil.

I paced the floor continuing in prayer all night. At 7:00 a.m., the phone rang. It was my daughter. Hearing her whimpering and her voice cracking, I knew why she had called before she said anything. She had received a phone call from Lee's best friend at work. He had found Lee slumped over his desk with a gun lying on the floor. She confirmed my fears; Lee had shot himself around 3:30 a.m.

Later that afternoon, there was a knock on my door. Opening the door slowly, I recognized the mail carrier standing there. He handed me Lee's wallet, rings, and watch and said, "I found these in your mailbox and thought you might want them."

Shutting the door, I braced my body against the wall and almost got sick to my stomach. The bloodshed from last night could have easily turned into a murder and suicide. God protected and led me out of the path of death's door.

All in all, suicide is a selfish act; it leaves the people it touches second-guessing what they might have done differently and brings suffering to the survivors.

One in four women will experience domestic violence during her lifetime. The lingering effects of domestic abuse are depression, anxiety, and emotional distress. Things will not change unless victims speak up and speak out. Sufferers of domestic violence need to know there is help available.

My experience with domestic violence is over 15 years old. Since then, I have distanced myself from the turmoil, but the experience made me understand better the ugliness of abuse and the aftereffects of suicide. God holds the keys to protection and shelter for the hurting. I now understand Him in a way I never had before.

I am now content to live a quiet, simple life. My biggest rush of excitement is to chase after God, therefore, I put my future in the name of the Lord and he gave me this verse to claim. "The name of the LORD is a fortified tower: the righteous run to it and are safe."

The Tower

I trust the owner of the tower by the sea;
He's the great Provider and Father to me.
Violent storms send me seeking shelter to hide,
The mighty tower is where my safety lies.

God is my protector and shields me from all harm;
He will fight my battles; no need for alarm.
In His consoling arms, I shall fear no more;

You can find the tower close by to the shore.

His refuge is sound and a secure place to be;
Everyone is welcome to come, stay, or flee.
Within the strong walls, eternal love abounds.
His fortified tower will never fall down.

Practical Steps

Later I learned the whys of such tragedies. Abusers need to be in control, even to the extent of setting the time of death for themselves or others.

Scene-By-Scene

Two years after Lee's death, I bought a second home as an investment for my retirement. The condo was a small, well-decorated end-unit in St. Simons Island, Georgia. The day of the closing, a girlfriend and I decided to go out and celebrate. I was so proud that I had added another feather to my hat. Joan and I wound up in a country bar in a nearby town. Walking inside this smoky establishment, I noticed I was standing beside a mechanical bull. My friend dared me to ride it, and I took the challenge. I went up to the young man helping people ride the bull and said, "I'm next! Please be gentle." I put the glove on my left hand, put my foot in the stirrup, and with the help of the young man, straddled the bull. As long as the bull was in slow motion, I stayed in the saddle. The performer inside me came alive and I decided to ham it up to get attention. I raised my left arm up and held on to the horn with my right. I noticed several people pointing to me and watching me ride the bull. The bull gained speed, and I flew off and landed flat on my back. I wobbled to my friend and smirked, "Did you notice all those people watching me?"

Joan said, "Linda, you had the glove on the wrong hand. Your left hand was in the air and your bare hand was holding onto the horn."

Embarrassed and nauseated, I couldn't get out of that establishment fast enough.

Later that week, I was trying to figure out what I could do in St. Simons part-time to keep me entertained and challenged, and to supplement my income after I retired. It so happened that Joan and I went to dinner at a local seafood restaurant where I noticed a sign that said, "Be a sea captain. U.S.C.G. accredited classes being offered in Brunswick, Georgia, to earn your captain's license." I thought to myself, *I can do that.* After all, I loved boating, and it would be another achievement to be a captain. Everyone would think I was a smart, exceptional woman. Today I realize I was a foolish, self-focused woman.

I wasn't self-determined; I was self-destructive. I was always striving to earn someone's approval or a pat on the back. I didn't know it at the time, but what I needed was God's approval.

My goal was to retire at fifty, but it took time to get my affairs in order so at fifty-four I planned a going-out-of-business sale one weekend and organized a home estate sale the next week. One day while packing a few photos and preparing to close the studio, a thought hit me right in the gut, or maybe it was a nudge from the Holy Spirit: I had never taken the time to dance before the Lord. I knew my relationship with the Lord had encountered its highs and lows, but this might be my last chance to dance just for Him. After all, God had protected me and my business over the years. I silenced the phones, locked the doors, and turned the music as loud as I could to the song of *I Can Only Imagine.* As I danced for an audience of One, I felt so alive, so thankful. My spirit quickly filled with emotions of laughter and tears. That dance moved my relationship with God from something "out there" to someone in my very being. I finally recognized blessings for what they are and praised the Father for them. I had a sign hung in my office at the studio that said *Dance like nobody is watching. Sing like nobody is listening. Love like you have never been hurt, and live like it is Heaven on Earth.* On that day I executed Psalms 150: "Let them praise His name with dancing and make music to him with timbrel and harp."

The dance I performed before the Lord started the transformation from being a self-absorbed, self-willed, it's-all-about-me dancer to a woman that desired to know Christ better. Self-absorption is a choice, and I wanted God's vision for my life. Dancing with the feet is one thing, but dancing with the heart is another. It was time to say goodbye to a business that dominated me.

It takes time and work to change bad habits and old thinking. The evil one is in a battle for our minds and choices. Most days I miss the mark. God only wants me to do my best. He will handle my shortcomings. I believe that is why God allows me to fall short now and then. When I operate in my human strength, I can only accomplish human size results.

During the time I was going to sea school, my sister Andrea asked me to ride down to Gulf Shores, Alabama with her to take a break and check out the area. I knew the long car ride would allow me time to study for my captain's license, so I decided to take her up on her offer. After we arrived at the coast of Alabama, I took one look at the waterways and knew this was where I wanted to hang up my hat for the rest of my days. Within twenty-four hours, I bought two condos. One was on Plash Island which is in the far northwest corner of Gulf Shores, and the other was in Orange Beach which is the town just east of Gulf Shores. I had owned the home in St. Simons for less than two years and was surprised it sold so quickly. Six weeks later I made my last trip to South Georgia to pack up a few things and say my goodbyes.

I could only imagine God's plans were on the Alabama Gulf Coast.

Keep Dancing: Bill

Bill and I were playing cards with another couple. We were making small talk, and Ruth asked me, "Are you daydreaming?"

I responded, "I'm sorry, my mind was wandering, as usual."

"Well, don't leave us in the dark. What were you thinking?" Charles asked, with a mischievous grin.

Shuffling the cards, I said, "An amazing thing happened yesterday, during my quiet time with the Lord I had a feeling He was whispering, *Write about your life.*" Everyone laughed. Then Charles snickered, "Would your husband be mentioned?"

With an exaggerated sigh, I answered, "Of course. Bill's my spouse and we share everything! We just disagree on some things." My friends were darting glances at each other because they knew we had blended families and different religious beliefs.

After our guests left, I rested in bed pondering how many loved ones, friends, and neighbors didn't have a relationship with Jesus. *Many*, I thought, and I finally fell asleep.

The next morning, Bill was reading his email. I asked, "Am I disturbing you?"

He turned to look at me with a raised eyebrow, "No. What can I do for you, my dear?"

I told him, "I want to write about relationships and how I have learned from them. I want to show how love can be restored and hurts can be healed. I also want to write about our marriage with different beliefs on Christianity."

To my relief, he said, "I think that's an excellent idea. Other people are just like us. Go for it!" The conversation was simple and straightforward.

With a twinkle in his eye and a nod of his head, I had Bill's approval and the freedom to begin.

Finding the Right Partner

Scuba diving the Grand Cayman Wall has always been on my bucket list. I finally had the opportunity while vacationing in the Caribbean with my mother and sister. They both declined when I asked them to join me, so I booked the excursion for one. When we departed, I felt alone, even though the boat held twenty participants. Couples helped each other, strapping on their tanks, talking and laughing. It was hard not to notice their happiness as I turned to the job of putting my gear on by myself. However, once I dove into the water and saw God's beauty, my loneliness dissipated. Feeling weightless and released from the sounds of above, I began to feel refreshed and thankful for this opportunity. The return ride to the port, though, brought sadness as the couples enjoyed each other and described the wonders they had seen below the surface. I had no one. It had been seven years since my divorce, and loneliness filled my heart. It was then I made the decision to find someone to share my life. After I returned home, I met Bill. I was ready to take another chance at love. Let me share our love story.

The Attraction

Eight years after my divorce from Lee, I met Bill. Meeting him reminds me of the lyrics to Lee Ann Womack's song, "I Hope You Dance": *Livin' might mean takin' chances but they're worth takin'; lovin' might be a mistake but it's worth makin'; and when you get the choice to sit it out or dance.....I hope you dance.*

During my life, I have embraced the thought that it is better to lose at love than never love at all. Bill gave me another chance to get love right. We are relational beings from birth, and it's interesting throughout life to discover new approaches to connect with others.

Bill and I began dating in October, 2003. We got acquainted on a dating website. He was a widower and had lost his wife of thirty-four years in a car accident. I was the second woman he had dated after grieving for five years. The attraction between us was our love of boating. After several dates, he took me to Carters Lake Marina, in the North Georgia Mountains to check out his 1978 Chris Craft classic cruiser. I stepped onto this ageless beauty, and Bill gave me a tour and a ride. We talked about our dreams and beliefs, and I learned he was agnostic, but that wasn't important to me at the time. Bill was charming, intelligent, and a gentleman. Spending time with him was fun, and those were the things that mattered.

After a sizzling summer I passed the coast guard test and returned to Dalton to register students and staff for the next season.

One Sunday night, I asked Bill to accompany me to my church's Christmas performance. As I sat beside him and glanced his way he showed no emotion. Afterward, he said, "The presentation was entertaining with all the glitz and glamour." I thought that was an odd thing to say about a stage play representing the birth of Jesus. Church and God weren't high on my priority list at this time, so I let the comment slide and continued to play the dating game.

Four months later, I realized Bill was serious about our relationship, and we talked about marriage. He surprised me with a trip to San Francisco. He knew I would like the scenic shorelines, Alcatraz Island, Fisherman's Wharf, and the water adventures the seaside cultural center had to offer. Bill made reservations for dinner at a romantic restaurant with a view of the bay area and the Golden Gate Bridge. He seemed nervous throughout dinner. As soon as we finished dessert he suggested we head back to the hotel. In our room, Bill pulled out a chair and with a serious look on his face said, "Please sit down." On one knee, he took a box from his jacket pocket, and opened it to reveal a diamond ring. "Will you marry me?" he asked.

I caught my breath and looked at his anxious face. I wanted to wait but, said, "Yes." He slid the ring on my trembling finger, and we set our wedding date.

The Wedding Day

Ten months later, on a cold day in December, we hosted an intimate gathering of family, adult children, and friends in a charming dining room in a quaint establishment called The Woodbridge Inn, located on the gentle hills of Jasper, Georgia. I waltzed toward Bill in a red velvet dress, sweating profusely. In the back of my mind, I worried we were making a mistake. I held Bill's trembling hands while our guests looked on. Outside, shimmering white snowflakes were falling; deer were prancing in the open fields behind the restaurant. I thought to myself. "What a beautiful background for my wedding day!" While reciting vows to each other, Bill's voice choked with tears. Next, the minister quoted from Ecclesiastes, "Two can accomplish more than one, for the results can be much better." As soon as we were pronounced man and wife, I wondered if it would be hard for me to give up my independence and what would be different in making this commitment work.

Making Adjustments

Our first year was exciting! We honeymooned in Aruba, launched a cruise business named SunRay Cruises, and started to build a new home in Alabama. In our hectic schedules, we didn't have time to think about whether our marriage was good or bad. They say the first year is the hardest, but we were too busy to notice! Being consumed with days of activity was also an excuse not to attend church. We worked on Sundays, taking passengers to tour the southern Alabama waterways. Two years into the cruise business, we weren't making enough money to keep the company afloat. We decided to stop offering cruises and start planning weddings that would be held on our property where we were constructing our new home. I loved playing the role of a wedding coordinator, and we averaged forty weddings a year. Bill was the photographer and webmaster for our Weddings by the Bay. We were constantly answering the phone, showing potential customers our property, or preparing for one of our client's weddings. At the same time, we were trying to complete construction on our house and deal with all the contractor problems such a project entails.

I loved entertaining and helping couples have the wedding they always wanted. Each wedding reminded me of past dance recitals. After a thirty plus years in the dance business, I could put on a show with my eyes closed. It was all about the production and making the bride happy. Bill couldn't have cared less about the business. He didn't like having strangers on the property and he only consented to the partnership until I could draw Social Security. We found ourselves fighting up to the time each wedding party arrived. Instead of complementing each other, we were always bickering about which one of us worked harder. Arrogance, lack of communication, devaluing each other, and using control—each of those faults was destroying our marriage.

I hounded Bill until he agreed to put a hold on finishing the house so we could concentrate on the wedding business and soon fell back to my old habits of being consumed by pleasing customers first and family second. Winter months were the slow season for weddings, so we took this opportunity to travel, but I couldn't enjoy our vacations for fear I would miss a phone call or email from a bride-to-be. For example, we were on a 21-day cruise from Rome to South Africa—a once in a lifetime vacation for both of us. Instead of enjoying my alone time with Bill and appreciate being pampered, I complained about the Wi-Fi not working.

When I finally found a hotspot, I couldn't wait to read my emails. I would open the submission forms from potential brides first. When the Wi-Fi kicked off, I would turn to Bill, patiently sitting beside me, waiting for his turn to use the laptop and scream, "I am so tired of being on this crappy ship that doesn't have a decent signal for the internet!"

He didn't understand why I was taking it out on him, so he would yell back, "It's not my fault! Get over it!"

I didn't want to get over it; I wanted to respond to the inquiry. I told Bill, "If I don't show an interest and reply to the emails, we will lose the clients and they will go somewhere else to have their wedding." Bill just shrugged his shoulders and walked off cussing under his breath. I yelled after him, "You don't give a flip, do you?" Feeling like I was the only one that wanted to be successful in Weddings by the Bay, I hurried to our cabin, grabbed my swimsuit and stayed at the pool by myself the rest of the day.

Later that year, without asking Bill, I made the mistake of accepting a wedding and reception on December 31st. I thought it would be fun and being a holiday, we charged extra. The contract stated the wedding party was to leave the premises fifteen minutes after midnight.

At 12:10, I found Bill sitting in his comfortable chair in the living room and told him, "Everyone is having a festive time, so I am going to let our guests stay longer at no extra charge."

He replied, "No you're not. I will turn the lights off." Minutes later, he turned out the lights and huffed off.

Pretending, nothing was wrong I quickly turned the lights back on and apologized to the remaining guests. I was embarrassed, and my insides were in a rage over what Bill had done.

Before the groom left, he complained we rushed the bridal party and the guests. He demanded part of his money back. I had to handle the situation all by myself. I stayed up the rest of the morning to clean the reception area and wash the dishes and tablecloths. I wanted to make sure Bill knew I didn't need him and that he wasn't pulling his weight as a partner in business or marriage. I remembered the minister saying, "A man shall leave his father and mother and be joined to his wife, and they shall become one flesh," but, I felt alone. I knew I could run this business without him. I had no intention of changing my need to control.

After the New Year's Eve incident, I couldn't get rid of my bad feelings toward my husband. I called a girlfriend and asked her to have lunch. I confided that it was difficult adjusting as a married couple. With a worried look, my friend said tenderly, "If you don't work on relationships, you lose them." Her words tugged at my heart. Feeling uneasy, I went home to discuss my attitude toward Bill and the New Year's

Eve incident. Needless to say, we wound up in an argument over who worked harder, which one of us was contributing more money to the household, and who caused the most problems. I went to bed irritated. For three days we didn't speak to each other or make eye contact.

A few days later, I was carrying clean laundry to the upstairs bedroom when Bill and I bumped into each other on the stairs. I asked him, "Do you remember what we were fighting about?"

He hesitated. Then, with a blank look on his face, he said, "No, I don't have a clue!"

I wanted to get this settled, so in an apologetic tone I said, "I'm sorry if you're sorry." As I put the laundry away, I couldn't believe we wasted time on a matter that he couldn't even remember.

A few years went by and we were still adjusting to married life. We got married in our golden years so we decided to renew our vows and have a party to celebrate our fifth anniversary. Our children didn't understand and said they had never heard of a couple renewing their vows on their fifth year. We laughed and explained that, at our age, we might not be around to celebrate our 25th. The event was held at our home on a chilly evening around dusk. I wore a black dress with a silver wrap. Bill looked handsome in black pants, white sports jacket, and a dark gray shirt with a silver tie. We wrote our vows to each other. Bill spoke briefly about the journey with each other and I rambled about how he was a gift from God. To the outside world, we seemed like the perfect couple in a perfect setting, but in reality, I felt neglected and unfulfilled.

The wedding business lasted seven years; Bill initially agreed to five seasons, but I kept pushing to book more weddings. He wasn't a happy husband or business partner. When I had booked three weddings on a Saturday in October, he said forcefully, "I have had it! It's either me or the wedding business!"

I knew he was serious. I looked up at his tired face and said, "Bill, I choose you."

He agreed to fulfill our obligations for the scheduled weddings. At first, his attitude and demeanor changed, but soon, Bill and I were getting on each other's nerves again because I stayed on the go and he was happy to be home. I would like to talk, and he wanted quiet. We didn't have the same interest in television programs or going to church. We bickered constantly, and I desperately needed validation. Therefore, I made a special effort to fix steak stir-fry one evening——Bill's favorite. I went to the grocery store and bought all the best ingredients. After I got home, I realized I had picked up the wrong soy sauce. I made another trip to the store and decided to make his preferred dessert too. It took me hours to get everything ready. After I pulled the chocolate chip pound cake out of the oven, I told myself it would be worth it. I arranged the table with his family china that had been stored in the attic. For a last minute touch, I put cut flowers from the garden on the table and lit candles to set the romantic mood.

We sat down to eat, and I waited anxiously to hear Bill's comments. After a few bites, my heart was racing. I grabbed his arm and asked, "Well? What do you think?"

He replied, "The meat is fatty and hard to chew. Why did you use broccoli instead of snap peas? I can do a lot better at stir-fry than you can. We're not having guests, why did you bother with the china and candles?"

That wasn't what I wanted to hear. My efforts were meaningless. I swallowed hard and said, "I can't do anything right. I'm going for a drive." I grabbed the car keys before he could make another hurtful remark and hurried outside. Pausing at a stop sign, gripping the steering wheel a little too tightly, I wondered what would happen if I kept on driving, never to return home. I was considering a separation, but God had other plans. In the next instant, I turned the wheel and headed home. I desperately wanted a happy marriage. The decision to go back wasn't hard; letting go of my pride was! There was no doubt in my mind I was partially to blame for the sad state of our marriage. I had a destructive habit of controlling behavior and didn't know how to fix it. I was trying to operate on my own strength and poured out my aching heart to God, praying that He would show me how to turn my marriage around.

About the same time, a Mobile pregnancy center where I had been a volunteer offered a healing class to help overcome confining areas in one's life. I signed up for the class, and the first thing I learned was about *strongholds*. Scripture says in 2 Corinthians 10:3-4, "We are human, but we don't wage war as humans do. We use God's mighty weapons, not worldly weapons, to knock down the strongholds of human reasoning and to destroy false arguments." The false arguments are the work of the deceiver, reminding us how worthless, dirty, and insignificant we are. The only weapon we have to defeat opposition is to use God's power.

Holding onto the truth of the Word, I wrote down all the names of people I had hurt in the past and in the present. I started with Coach and decided to write a letter describing how wrong I was to have used him. One by one, I called others who I had hurt or mislead. I sat and cried at my husband's feet, taking ownership of my manipulation and attempts to control him. I asked him for forgiveness for showing disrespect and discontent. I wasn't going to let the enemy throw more darts to destroy my relationship with my husband. The Biblical healing class had made me understand how I had hurt others, and showed me ways to heal those deeply-rooted hurts.

I became a better wife when I realized the choices we make now determine whether we will be happy later. Proverbs 14 says, "A wise woman builds her house, but the foolish tears it down with her own hand." It is impossible for me to read God's word, be in his presence, and not change. It seems obvious to me now, but it took years for me to get to this point. I began to think more about Bill than myself, and I demonstrated my love for Bill by putting his needs before mine. Bill realized something was different about me and our marriage.

For our tenth anniversary, we renewed our love at a marriage retreat. We left the retreat declaring our two hearts had one commitment. In the end, it's all about the commitment. I will continue to pray and ask God for wisdom because our marriage is healthier, and more secure than before. Martin Luther once said, "Let the wife make the husband glad to come home, and let him make her sorry to see him leave." That's the kind of relationship I want with my husband. When Bill comes home, he's happy to see me, not dreading an encounter with a controlling wife. Because of this new practice, we fall more in love every day and have respect within our home. I choose to relinquish control and have a greater level of peace in my marriage. For me, God is able, through His mighty power, to do more than we ask or think. Married couples need to know, even if we are complete opposites, that two can accomplish more than one on the dance floor of daily living. I have found for two people to dance together well, one must lead, and the other must follow. Opposites do attract. Equally important, love can be restored.

Love Can Turn Around

For better or worse, here's a real love story,
With different beliefs, will this union bring glory?
Their blame for each other always got in the way;
What a struggle for both just to get through the day.

Both looked for excuses to leave their marriage,
They forgot their vows to love, honor, and cherish.
When their love began on such a weak foundation,
No glimmer of hope in their sad situation.

Their love turned around; God is unstoppable!
He will heal all struggles that seem impossible.
A working marriage takes supreme authority,
The vows we make should be our top priority.

Practical Steps

Behind great dancers there are hard lessons that have been learned.

Imbalance

There is no relationship perfect on earth, but we can find ways to improve how we love.

One of the best gifts I ever received was from my husband on Mother's Day, 2008. It was a bright, clear morning, and I was trying to get ready for church. I was to speak representing a local pregnancy center for baby dedication day. Brushing my teeth, I could see Bill behind me in the bathroom mirror. He bolted out of bed with a broad grin and asked, "Would you like to open your gift now?"

"Not now, Hon, I'm trying to get ready for church and don't want to be late."

I hurried and got dressed while deciding what jewelry to wear.

Bill pleaded as he watched me get ready, "Open my gift before you leave!"

"As soon as I go downstairs," I said.

Putting on my high heels, I dashed down the steps, grabbed my Bible, and bolted for the door.

Passing Bill, I saw him shaking a small package wrapped in silver paper with a black satin bow. He called after me, "Come back, I think you forget something and would like to wear this today."

His last statement got my interest. Walking toward him, I snatched the present and hurried for the couch. I sat down and made eye contact with Bill, "I'm sorry it took so long for me to open your gift."

He was moving about like an excited child waiting for Christmas morning. I pulled the paper off and wadded it in a ball in my hand. Then I tossed the paper to the floor so I could tear open the box. I beheld an exquisite pearl and diamond cross on an embellished silver chain. I stood up and kissed his forehead. "It's beautiful! Will you help me?" I offered him the necklace, and Bill clasped it around my neck. I couldn't help feeling guilty that it took three times for him to ask me to open it.

Driving to church, I wondered if that is how God thinks humans view His Son. That somehow, Jesus has gotten lost in a pile of ribbon and wrapping, and His gift of salvation is thrown on the floor. I entered the sanctuary that Mother's Day in 2008 and sat down in one of the pews. The pastor called my name to speak about the sanctity of life. I picked up the cross Bill had given me earlier and thought how different things were in 2004 before we married. I had a new level of awareness of how blessed I was to have Bill as a husband and how blessed to be who I had become in Christ. My real happiness is serving God.

During my talk, I shared how life is precious to God. I also spoke about the pregnancy center and the opportunities available to help. After the service, I couldn't wait to go home and tell Bill, "I'm grateful for your love. Thank you for my Mother's Day gift."

At the end of the day, I thought of the gifts God had given me. They were part of His nature and a pure expression of His goodness. Since I have a personal relationship with Jesus, I might go astray, but my Lord is compassionate. When I cast my anxieties on Him, He cares for me. Nevertheless, I have found God's ultimate gift is His everlasting, never-failing love.

Gifts

Our good and perfect gifts come from above,
The Father of light shines His gracious love.
His presence beams in Heaven and on Earth,
Ready to bless all, beginning with birth.

God's character will always stay the same,
Human beings want His power and fame
Our God-given talents are not our own
Pride in us says, "We did it all alone."

Practical Steps

To keep good balance in life, I must focus on my relationships with God and family.

Jesus in a Box

Bill and I decided a few years back to clean out our master bedroom closet and make it more efficient. I had accumulated dozens of outfits including several that still sported tags. I counted twenty-five boxes of shoes. There were various hat boxes with summer and winter headgear. Smaller purses were stuffed inside large designer pocketbooks to save space on the shelves. My deprived husband would be lucky to have twenty percent of the closet, and I complained I didn't have room for all my wardrobe and accessories. Despite my vast collection of clothing, I gazed inside my closet that morning and couldn't find a thing that made me happy to wear. I finally settled for one of my retired dance t-shirts and a pair of sweatpants.

I was ready to remove the clutter and decided to start with the shoes. Standing on my toes, I reached for the top box, and it fell to the floor, tumbling into a corner. I took the remaining four boxes to the hall, then sorted them into piles—keep, throw away, and give away. Going back to retrieve the fallen box triggered a memory of when I stuffed Jesus inside a box and kept Him in my closet, taking Him out only in desperate situations when He was useful to me. I shook the thought from my head and continued working.

My goal was to throw out anything that I hadn't worn in the last few years. It wasn't easy to toss my stuff, since I still had days when I slid back into trying to impress people. While sorting through a few sweaters, I found an old metal box. I picked it up and dusted it off. I slowly walked to the bed bench chewing my bottom lip. I sat down and tapped the container with my eyes closed trying to remember what was in it.

After a few minutes, I couldn't stand it any longer and quickly opened it. The first thing I saw were some blue and red ribbons and gymnastic medals. Rummaging through the box, I realized it was where I kept all my accomplishments—a pride box. I was sorting through the certificates and papers when I eyed a letter on aqua stationery. My eyes widened as I reread the letter postmarked 1967 from Weeki Wachee Springs in Central Florida. I had applied for a position at the amusement park which featured live mermaids dancing under water, and the letter welcomed me to audition. Performing there had been my teenage dream; even at age fifty-six, I had asked that my grandchildren call me *Mermaid* rather than *Grandma*.

Next, I saw ribbons earned following various contests. If I had room in my pride box for the crowns and trophies I had won, I would have crammed them in there too, but those had been stored in an attic. Eventually, over time, the crowns and trophies tarnished to a dull black, and I had to throw them away. My heart ached when I saw the rewards discarded like old pairs of shoes.

I realized that my relationship with Jesus was similar to how I had stored my awards. I abandoned Jesus for all those years, putting Him in a box when I was too caught up in the world and what it offered. Old habits are hard to die.

I know now Jesus can't be boxed in or figured out. He will not dance to human expectations. He allowed me to experience my will. Salvation was my first gift, but it doesn't give me a free pass not to grow spiritually. The gift of transformation took me longer to unwrap and understand. When I see myself slipping back into long established habits, I pray that God will help me with my spiritual growth. A Christian life is a process. I depend on God to show me what's important. He's showing me my value is not in how much stuff I have. Slowly I'm beginning to clean out excess things in my life that weigh me down. It makes me happy to have more time for family, friends, and God.

Apostle Paul says it best in 1 Thessalonians 2. "After all, what gives us hope and joy, and what will be our proud reward and crown as we stand before our Lord Jesus when he returns? I live by faith in the Son of God, who gave himself for me." Jesus died for me on that old rugged cross. I will cherish and cling to the cross until, at last, I lay my trophies down. Some day, I hope to exchange them for a crown. Today, I cling to the cross and don't want clothes, crowns, or trophies to be my idols. The Bible says in Ecclesiastes 1:2, "Everything is completely meaningless!" I have turned my accumulation of stuff over to Christ. Clutter distracted me and stressed me out. I have been set free from the bondage of material objects. Jesus is my joy and hope. Nothing else matters, and that is when real transformation begins.

The Box

I started the day feeling all alone,
Fear of the future and all that's unknown.
In the master closet, I found a heart shaped box,
Curious of its contents like a sly ole fox.

Printed on the lid was, *Please open me,*
I wondered if I should let the box be.
Deep breathing allowed me to settle down and cope,
I tore the box open with a heart full of hope.

Inside was a note the color of blood,
You are my child that I surely love.

Your life story is supposed to shine like a star,
I have always been near to you, never too far.

My Spirit is with you throughout the day,
Pulling you close so you won't get away.
Give me your broken dreams so I can lift you high,
Keep your focus on me where victory can rise.

We don't communicate, and I want more,
For you to depend on me like before.
Falling tears tumbled as I continued to read,
I am your caring Father, permit me to lead.

Believing in God, I can't go astray,
The box on the table showed me the way.
Somehow I forgot to give my burdens to Him,
With the Father holding me, I will always win.

Practical Steps
Every day, look to God to find the right balance.

Walking Together Through the Valley of Cancer

After thirty-eight years of either being married to a man, or married to a business, or both, I reevaluated my actions and life.

Bill and I made plans to vacation in the Western Caribbean for our tenth anniversary before his voice began to develop a rasping sound. We had concerns, but felt it would be better to deal with the problem after some warm weather and togetherness. On the third day of the cruise, I left an anniversary card on the cabin dresser for Bill. I included brochures about a couple's marriage retreat I had scheduled for us for Valentine's Day weekend. Bill read the card then looked at the pamphlets. He glanced quickly at them and asked despairingly, "Is this one of those *Christian* events?"

I smiled, took a deep breath, and whispered, "Yes. If you choose to go, it will make me very happy. Think of it as an investment in the future. If some reason you don't like the retreat, we can drop the classes." Reluctantly, he agreed.

For the rest of the cruise, we rested and did not talk about Bill's strained voice. After we returned to Gulf Shores, Bill made an appointment for a biopsy. A few days later we got the results.

We weren't shocked when they told us the biopsy indicated stage-one cancer, because Bill had been a smoker most of his life. Beginning February 17th, 2015, Bill would have 33 radiation treatments over a six-week period. The prognosis was good, and people were praying for him. The oncologist said the growth was in an easy area to remove. Thessalonians 5:18 says," Give thanks in all things," so I gave thanks that we had enough insurance, the doctor found it early, and the position of the cancer was in an area to have a full recovery. My mother would always tell me, "You can always find something good in the awful."

Bill and I wanted to get his cancer diagnosis behind us so we could move on with our lives. If you stay in the mud, you get stuck. A quote from tough guy Winston Churchill said it all: "If you're going through hell, keep going."

As we prepared for the surgery our Valentine's get-a-way marriage retreat arrived quickly. We checked into our hotel and found the conference center. Our first class featured games for us to play to make marriage fun. We played a puzzle game to see who could put the pieces together first. Bill and I put our heads together to be the first ones to finish. We didn't win, but the purpose was to show us, two are better than one in life. In the second game, each used ropes to restrain his or her blindfolded partner, and then, without words, had to help the partner figure out how to get loose. The lesson we learned was to depend on each other when we are in binding situations. Bill enjoyed the subject and challenges. After the lecture, he mentioned, "That wasn't bad at all, and the best part was there wasn't any preaching."

We decided to skip the next session and go for an early romantic dinner overlooking the Destin Harbor. Before we left the conference, we agreed we would return for the seven o'clock praise and worship concert. Standing together in the auditorium, I was clapping, and singing, having a sweet time when Bill nudged me and said, "This is too much. Let's go." I followed him to the car in silence. I prayed that when I spoke my heart would not show my discouragement.

The next day I woke Bill up gently saying, "Good morning, how did you sleep, Love?"

In a playful mood, he muttered, "Super."

I teased him, "If we take classes this morning, you can choose the sessions, and I'll buy you lunch." He agreed and picked up the class schedule on the night stand.

With a grin on his face, he said, "Let's go to the class called *Intimacy*."

I winked and said, "You got it."

We dressed and hurried to class. As we got there, a couple was sharing with the class how they prayed for each other. They said, "Praying together creates caring and tenderness. If, for some reason, praying aloud feels awkward, try praying silently."

Check-out time was 11:00, so we decided to pack up our belongings, leave the conference early, and stop for lunch on the way home. Thoughts of praying with Bill kept burning in my mind since we never had done this. When we arrived at the restaurant, I asked Bill, "Would you like to pray silently with me before each radiation treatment? I have prayed for you for years. Sometimes it would be nice for you to pray with me."

He blinked and muttered, "Sure."

I gave him a big kiss and thanked God under my breath.

Soon after we returned home, Bill started his treatments at the cancer treatment center. Every time before he left for his procedures, we held hands and prayed silently.

A few weeks went by, and I ended my prayers earlier than usual and caught him looking around the room as if he was bored. I quickly asked Bill, "Do you seek God during those moments we pray together?"

"No, I don't. Remember, I don't pray."

With an aggravated tone and my hands on my hips, I asked, "Is this wasting your time? Do you want to continue?"

He replied "No, don't stop! It lets me know you care."

"Hum," I remembered several friends that don't believe in the power of prayer, but when I asked them if I could pray for them, not one said, "No, I don't need your prayers." My Bible tells me in James 5, "The earnest prayer of a righteous person has great power."

I turned to face my husband with a warm smile and said, "No problem, and, yes, I do care." The next morning before Bill left for his treatment, I prayed while he stood beside me. Afterwards, when the house was all mine, I had time to reflect. I enjoy my quiet time with the Lord, because it renews my body, mind, and spirit, and I have found is the key to Christian living.

Cancer affects many people and lives. It has a rippling effect. Although Bill experienced the cancer, I experienced what caregivers go through. In marriage we are two separate human beings, but we have one goal, a shared purpose. The Bible says in Ecclesiastes 4:12, "Though one may be overpowered, two can defend themselves." God created marriage and joined man and woman together. The bond that God has tied together is not to be lightly untied. I trust in His mighty work and path for my life. Bill follows self. I am on the narrow road hearing the voice of God saying '"Trust me." Matthew 7 tells me, "Small is the gate and narrow the road that leads to life and only a few find it." Bill is walking on the wide road making his decisions his way. I have a new awareness of what God wants and expects of me. I will hold Bill's hand until death pulls us apart. Isn't that what human relationships are all about? My faith helped me to cope with Bill's cancer. I tell Bill all the time, "I have enough faith for both of us."

King David tells us in Psalm 23:4 that even though he walked through the darkest valley, he was not afraid when God, the Good Shepherd, walked at his side. Those words bring me comfort when I'm facing adversity. When I'm staring at a mountain, it consoles me to know someone will climb the uphill journey with me. No one is immune to life's struggles.

Life's Struggles

Lord, supply my needs in the midst of silence;
Humbly I come before you; praying for guidance.
To carry burdens is highly demanding.
I don't want to lean on my own understanding.

Lead me to still waters where peace overflows,
I will feel no evil, that's how the story goes.
Suffering and pain will always be around,
Send your comfort as I lay my struggles down.

Life has twists and turns, but you are in control,
As I walk through the valleys you restore my soul.
God cares about me and the despair in my heart,
His love for His children will never depart.

Practical Steps

Despite our past struggles or present situation, we are not alone.

Practice Makes Perfect

My cousin Paul and his wife Brenda came to visit on Labor Day Weekend, 2015. My husband Bill and I prepared for their arrival. I cleaned the house, stripped the beds, and organized the meals. Bill put the finishing touches on the new boat lift he had built, making sure everything worked properly. All the details were completed and we waited anxiously for our houseguests.

My relatives arrived late Friday afternoon. Being a beautiful evening, we made the decision to take the boat and go to a local restaurant for dinner, asking another couple from the neighborhood to join us. When we returned home, we talked into the wee hours of the morning. It was a great time of catching up and loving family and friends.

Walking upstairs to get ready for bed, I realized I had not stopped to read God's word that day or to thank Him. I shrugged off the thought.

Early the next morning, I tidied up, washed a few dishes, put the coffee on, and fixed breakfast. It turned out to be a sunny day, so during breakfast we decided to drive 20 miles to Fort Morgan and take the ferry to Dauphin Island.

Once the boat pulled into port, we drove off the ferry, to my favorite southern town in Alabama—Fairhope—and took in all the sights.

Later, returning to Gulf Shores, we picked up some groceries, and I made dinner. Everyone was having a relaxing, fun time—everyone but me! I was too busy in the kitchen and resented Bill for not helping. I couldn't throw together something simple or order a pizza—I had to go all out and fix a gourmet meal to prove a point about my abilities. After dinner, I cleaned up, and I felt tired and aggravated with myself for doing too much. I quickly said my good nights and deliberately didn't kiss my husband. Climbing the stairs to our bedroom, I remembered it was the second day in a row that I hadn't taken the time to be alone with God.

On Sunday morning, the third day of Paul and Brenda's visit, I nudged Bill to get up. As he turned over, I asked in a sarcastic voice, "Are you ever going to get up? It's almost time to leave for church."

He sat up and said, "It's only 9:00 a.m."

I asked him, "Will you attend Bible study today? Paul and Brenda said they wanted to go."

His answer was always the same. "I only go to church to support you, not for the message. If something happened to you, I would never step into a church again. No, I don't want to go to Bible study."

The three of us left in Paul's car.

Worship on the Water is a Bible-based Christian congregation that meets in a tent at the famous Flora-Bama bar which sits on the Gulf of Mexico and spans the border between Florida and Alabama. It all started with a dare of, "Who would attend church in a bar?" Since the first service in 2011, the congregation has reached more than one hundred thousand people. I began attending with that first service, and for a couple of years, I have led the ladies' Bible group. The church holds two services—one in the morning at nine and the other at eleven o'clock. Between services we hold small group study and extra activities.

Bill met us right before the second worship.

While sitting in church that Sunday, singing the songs from the honky-tonk hymnal, I was secretly hoping to find my joy again. I knew I had overworked myself, and when our bodies are weary, we become irritable. Being busy not only steals my energy, but it also destroys my testimony. Somehow, I had lost it in the last twenty-four hours. Everybody else at church was excited. Our new pastor, Dan Stone, was going to preach his first sermon.

Unfortunately, I didn't catch the waves of excitement. I was annoyed at my husband and knew I was sliding into the poor-pitiful-me pit. I wondered why things didn't go the way I wanted. Try as I might, I couldn't relate to the pastor's message on family. I kept thinking *this is the message I have to talk about next week at Bible study*. Again, I was more concerned with how my performance would go than I was with learning something from the pastor. As much as I tried, I just couldn't shake my feelings. Every time my husband glanced my way, I turned my head.

Tapping me on the shoulder, Bill said, "I'm going to leave church early."

"Why?" I whined.

"It's Labor Day weekend, and the restaurants will fill up quickly after church."

"Go then," I said impatiently.

When Bill got up to leave Paul asked, "Is he going to the kneeling bench?"

Being in a self-righteous mood, I shrugged my shoulders.

After service, we met Bill for lunch. I had developed a headache, so I didn't eat my meal. When the waiter brought the check, I asked him for a takeout box. Bill had no problem consuming his food; except two small morsels of tuna. When the waiter brought the box, Bill asked, "Can I put my tuna in your box?"

I said too quickly, "Get your own carry out box."

Being drained was not an excuse for being selfish. I knew he would want to eat his leftovers later. We both left the restaurant not speaking.

After we got home, tension filled the air. The men watched football in silence, and Brenda and I took naps. I was simply worn out physically and emotionally. I should have taken the time to pray for grace and my family, but I didn't.

Following our nap and an afternoon of football, I suggested an early evening cruise. Bill thought it might rain and wanted to check the weather. After thirty minutes of waiting for him to get off the computer, I said in a blaring voice, "Okay, everyone; let's go for our boat ride while the coast is clear. I can maneuver the boat if Bill doesn't want to go."

Bill hung his head in disbelief. I had crossed the line, disrespecting my husband. My pride was bigger than honoring his wishes.

My cousin and his wife grabbed their sunglasses, hats, and water bottles. I had turned one last time before I dashed outside saying, "I sure wish you would join us, Bill."

With his eyebrows knitted together, he said, "Okay, then!"

The tension in the house followed us onto the boat. I couldn't wait for our cruise to be over so I could email my fellow Bible teachers to tell them I couldn't possibly facilitate the next week's lesson on family. To be honest, at that moment my relationships were imperfect and my husband didn't understand me.

Monday was Labor Day and we had invited other friends to cruise the waterway to the Orange Beach Wharf, eat lunch, walk around, and enjoy the activities. We were half way to the Wharf when I walked over to the captain's seat and told Bill, "Let me take the wheel and you rest for a while."

He chuckled and said, "Who? You? The woman who monopolizes all conversations? I don't think you can talk and pilot this boat at the same time."

Everyone laughed. Bill had made a joke about me, and I didn't appreciate it one bit. I remained silent the rest of the cruise.

Once we arrived at the Wharf, Bill and I decided to order oysters. He said, "Let's split a dozen."

I said, "I want my own dozen."

Apparently that upset him, and he said, "I split menu items with you all the time. Why is this problem?"

I repeated myself, "I want my dozen, and I'm hungry!"

Needless to say, we didn't speak another word during lunch. When everyone wanted to walk the Wharf, Bill said, "Go ahead. I'll stay here and watch the boat."

After we returned home, we made the best of it and played cards with our relatives and friends.

The next day Paul and Brenda got up early to leave. We sent them off with smiles and hugs. As we waved goodbye, I wondered if they knew Bill and I had fussed the last few days. When their car left the driveway, I turned to Bill and said, "We need to talk."

Entering the house and sitting down I blurted out, "What happened this weekend? How dare you tell my family that I couldn't talk and drive the boat at the same time?" I knew I was being prideful but couldn't help myself. Something in me wanted to argue. I was trying to communicate and confront this issue, knowing from past experiences if strife is ignored, it will not go away.

Bill blurted out, "You're too sensitive. What about last Sunday when you wouldn't let me put the few pieces of tuna in your box?"

I said a little too loudly, "It is what it is."

Looking back, what I was doing was trying to control the conversation and Bill. Nothing works right in life or relationships when you're dominating another person.

Our conversation had ended. I grabbed my Bible, leaving Bill sitting there. I headed to my prayer chair in a tucked away corner in the house where I could be alone with God. I needed wisdom and knew I wasn't walking in it. I wanted to be refreshed, to gain strength, and to try to find balance in my life. As soon as I sat down, I opened my Bible to Proverbs, the book of wisdom. Solomon wrote most of the Proverbs and asked God for wisdom. Guess what? God gave wisdom to him.

When you're in the family of God, Bible scriptures speak to you personally. I needed God to speak to me. I started studying the scriptures that Pastor Stone recited the previous Sunday—Ephesians 2: 19-20. I noticed my finger covering verse 14. Moving my hand away, I read, "For He Himself is our Peace." Boy, did I ever need peace that moment.

I opened my Bible to Psalm 10:11: "The wicked say to themselves, 'God isn't watching! He will never notice.'" As His child, I knew He was watching. I was ashamed of myself. Before I continued, I needed to stop and ask God for forgiveness for my attitude and the part that I played in this weekend's misery. Instantly, I was pulled out of my bad mood. Jesus' presence was near when I took the time to read His Word.

Jesus came to bring unity and harmony, not turmoil. We bring turmoil on ourselves. I needed to humble myself in front of God first, and then my husband. "God resists the proud but gives grace to the humble." (James 4:6)

The Bible contains many instructions about the family. God's words make us wise, wiser than our enemies. We need to apply this knowledge to change our everyday way of living. Therefore, I went to find Bill. He was hunched over the kitchen counter making a sandwich. I touched his hand and smiled, "Let me help you with that."

He replied, "Did your Bible reading deliver you from your bitchy disposition?"

I rubbed the back of my neck and said with a forced smile, "In fact, it did. I'm sorry my words were hateful the last few days."

Bill gave a heavy sigh and said, "I'm sorry too. Give me a hug."

Returning to my quiet spot I realized that when I first started feeling tired and unloved, I should have grabbed my Bible and read His instructions, not trusted my own feelings. When His words enter your heart, they help you to understand that the enemy wants to steal your joy and peace.

The Message Bible is a newer version of the Bible written in contemporary language that connects us right where we are in today's time. In Matthew 11 it says, "Are you tired? Worn out? Burned out on religion? Come to me. Get away with me and you'll recover your life. I'll show you how to take a real rest. Walk with me and work with me—watch how I do it. Learn the unforced rhythms of grace."

That insight needs to be learned intimately and practiced continuously. If our faith in Christ is real, it will prove itself anywhere we might be, especially at home. Peace is not a place; it's the One who delivers peace. Jesus says in Matthew 5:9, "God blesses those who work for peace, for they will be called the children of God." Partners must practice often to learn the steps that build connections so we don't step on each others toes.

Peace in the Home

Homes need to be filled with harmony and love,
Peace and unity comes from God above.

THE RELATIONSHIP DANCE

Does a stranger in your house lurk in the dark?
Pride in the home can tear couples apart.

God's children believes that Jesus is the way,
Belonging to Him gives us peace each day.
He gave the Bible as an instruction book,
It holds pages of wisdom; take a look.

Staying in the Word strengthens me as I go,
Making a difference in how my day flows.
Relationships shouldn't be an uphill test,
Lifting my burdens to God brings me rest.

High Hopes

Before we left for our journey to Israel, I asked a few of my prayer partners to pray for Bill's salvation. My exact words were, "Pray that his eyes be open." Friends told me they knew people who found Jesus in the Holy Land when they couldn't find Him anywhere else.

At long last, the moment I had waited for in Israel had arrived. It was the last day of our tour, and it was mid-afternoon. Perfect weather brought blue skies and a peaceful breeze. In Jerusalem, we were standing in the viewing area in the garden overlooking Calvary—literally, the place called the Skull. As I stood there, I visualized Jesus on His cross and the two thieves on each side. I could picture the crowd. His mother, friends, and the disciples were weeping and heartbroken. Others mocked Him—the soldiers performing their jobs and the multitude of bystanders. I have read and listened to the story many times; the difference this time was that the scene and sounds came alive. I tuned out the noises and conversations that surrounded me and imagined the voices the day Jesus was crucified. Immediately, I heard the pounding of nails into His flesh, insults hurled at Him, the words He uttered on the cross, the gasp of His last breath, the sound of the veil torn by the power of God, and the rattle of the earth shaking.

Before Jesus cried out, "It is finished," He was still thinking of others when He turned to one of the thieves and said, I tell you the truth, today you will be with me in paradise." Jesus' sinless life came to an end because of His love for sinful people.

Bill interrupted my thoughts as he grabbed my hand and said, "It's time to go to the burial site." The tomb is a rock-cut chamber. Some believe after Jesus was crucified, He was buried in this exact spot and raised to life, although another area in Jerusalem, the Church of Holy Sepulcher, also claims this honor.

I know it's difficult to pinpoint the location where historical events took place over two thousand years ago, but for me it's not about the exact position. I wanted to take home the memories, not dispute where these scenes took place.

Years ago, I told my husband if tomorrow it was proven that the Bible wasn't true or if Jesus wasn't who He said He was, I still would remain faithful in my belief. He is my hope that there is something far better than this fallen life. I heard my pastor say once, "If I am wrong, this world is the best it will ever be. If I'm right, this is the worst it will ever get."

Finally, we entered the tomb; it was a solemn moment for me standing in the burial place of my Lord and Savior. I turned to exit and looked at the opening of the cave. There I saw a plaque that read, *He is not here for He has risen*. My sadness instantly turned to happiness. I knew that the God I served was alive, had overcome death, and made a way for me to be in His presence forever.

Afterward, Bill and I walked to the gardens along with the rest of our touring friends. We sat in a circle feeling Jesus within our midst. Our group raised their voices and sang "Amazing Grace." We were fortunate to have two ministers in our group. Rev. Kathy Hartley stood up and told a story about Jesus being in agony, and how His sweat mixed with blood from his forehead fell like raindrops to the ground.

As soon as she finished, Pastor David Donaldson stood up and said, "I thought it would be meaningful to take communion together before we go our separate ways. The Pastor quoted scriptures from 1 Corinthians 11:23-29 (NIV), "The Lord Jesus, on the night he was betrayed, took bread, and when He had given thanks, He broke it and said, 'This is my body, which is for you; do this in remembrance of me.' In the same way, after supper he took the cup, saying, 'This cup is the new covenant in my blood; do this, whenever you drink it, in remembrance of me. For whenever you eat this bread and drink this cup, you proclaim the Lord's death until he comes.' So then, whoever eats the bread or drinks the cup of the Lord in an unworthy manner will be guilty of sinning against the body and blood of the Lord. Everyone ought to check themselves before they eat of the bread and drink from the cup. For those who eat and drink without discerning the body of Christ, eat and drink judgment on themselves."

I have heard these scriptures spoken in different churches and from various interpretations. To me, it's a sacred act to announce publicly that Jesus is the Son of God who died for me.

Meanwhile, as we passed the plate of bread and juice, baffled, I watched my husband take and consume the offering. I have never seen him participate in this ceremony before. In the past, he would excuse himself or pass the plate. Not only was I shocked but in a state of bliss, thinking he finally came to the conclusion Jesus was God in the flesh.

Afterwards, we hugged the other travelers goodbye and promised to keep in touch. As we were leaving Golgotha, the ministers requested a copy of my book when it was published. Mark, the tour director, overheard our conversation and asked about my book. I told him the book was about different beliefs and how that is woven into relationships.

Shaking Mark's hand, I said, "I wanted to take you to lunch to hear more about your faith, background, and story, plus ask a few questions. I felt you were busy taking care of everyone, so I didn't want to bother you."

Mark said, "Please send me the questions, and I promise to answer promptly."

Humbly, I said, "Thank you, Mark; you will never know how much this means to me."

The last words I remember him saying were, "I think you will be surprised with my answers about my Jewish beliefs."

Taking our seats on the bus, I told Bill, "You're never going to guess what happened? Mark told me to email him, and he would be glad to share his story and Jewish beliefs."

Bill said, "That will be interesting."

Our ride back to the hotel seemed like forever. I couldn't wait to be alone with Bill and ask why he took communion. I was contemplating how I was going to ask this question when I felt the Holy Spirit leading me to say nothing until Bill brought the subject up. I leaned against the bus window and closed my eyes thinking this was the best day of my life. Bill knew Jesus like I did.

Two days later, while we were packing to go back to the states, my curiosity got the best of me. I couldn't stand not knowing the details of the incident in the garden. I put aside what the Spirit had warned me, and lovingly asked Bill what happened.

I walked across the room and touched Bill's back and tenderly said, "I've never seen you take communion before. Did something happen while we were at Calvary? Have you changed your mind about who Jesus is?"

He stopped packing and turned to look at me, with a grin on his face, "Did you think that I have a new outlook on religion? Linda, I don't believe the way you do. Nor do I have your faith. Jesus was a good man, but no way is He the Son of

God. I'm sorry if you thought differently. I have never heard a pastor say that if I didn't believe, it would put my life in peril."

He continued. "For instance, you wouldn't pick up a coin lying on the ground if it was tails because you think it will bring bad luck. If it was heads, you would pick it up because you heard somebody once said it would bring good luck. It's all superstition. No person is going to tell me if I don't believe there will be a consequence. That is why I took communion."

After catching my breath, I struggled for composure. I never expected to hear what Bill said. I was upset and thought he had committed a horrible sin. Not knowing what to say next, I kept quiet to gather my thoughts and went to bed with terrible feelings toward my husband. I felt God's presence comfort me, and I was set free from being responsible for Bill's salvation.

The next morning, I wanted to put the incident behind me and was ready to fly back to the States. Fastening my seat belt, I prayed, "Lord, get us home."

Practical Steps

When challenges in life arise, I must do my best to maintain forward momentum.

Garden Grace

When I got back to Gulf Shores, I carried mixed emotions from my trip to Israel the week before. I called my closest friends to tell them we were safe and back home. I made a few comments about our Holy Land experience but kept what happened at the Garden Tomb a secret.

Three days later, I couldn't sleep, so I turned on the computer and started writing.

Bill woke up a couple of hours later, sat up in bed and asked, "What time did you get up? Are you writing about our footsteps of Christ tour?"

I continued typing and answered, "No, I'm not interested in writing about our trip to Israel."

"Why not?" he asked.

"Oh, Bill," I sighed. "You don't want me to write about what happened at the garden tomb for everyone to read." I stopped what I was doing and turned to face him hoping this wouldn't turn into an awkward conversation.

He jumped out of bed, took two full steps toward me and said, "I do! I want you to write about it, under one condition. If you write about me as an unbeliever, you need to write about Michael in our tour group who claimed to be a Christian. Do you remember what he said and did?"

"Hmmm. I don't have a clue what you're talking about."

"See how easily you overlook what you want to forget? Remember when Mark, our tour guide, took us to visit the fifteen hundred foot, mountain-top fortress of Masada where the last stronghold of the Jewish rebellion against the Roman invasion happened?"

Looking down, I replied, "Yeah."

"Michael, from our group, complained to the other tourists how unhappy he was. He shouted to Mark so that all on the bus could hear him, saying what a waste of time touring Masada was. It was an embarrassment to our Jewish friend. Those words hurt him, and none of the so-called Christians showed him any compassion. My dear, can't you see narrow-mindedness is still alive today in the Christian society?"

I couldn't imagine Michael's behavior had made such an impact on Bill and the way he thought about Christian followers. I stood up for my Christian brother, thrusting my chest out and said, "Mike probably wasn't even aware of his blunder."

Bill's comment confirmed what I have heard all my life: people are watching Christians actions and their words. We must control what comes out of our mouths.

Later on, we made the bed, and Bill said while fluffing the pillows, "That's why I left the church. Everyone fights over what they think and feel. It's malicious, and there's no victory for Christians in the end."

After Bill left, I paced the bedroom, stalling for time to mull over our discussion. I had a sinking feeling in my stomach and needed someone to talk to, so I called my friend Eleanor.

Later that afternoon, Eleanor and I took a walk around the neighborhood. We talked about writing then she came to an abrupt stop and asked, "Are you going to tell me about Israel?"

I started to feel dizzy and asked her if we could find a place to sit down.

After we found a soft grassy spot to sit, she asked, "What's wrong?"

With a false smile, I confessed to my friend that I had been upset with Bill since we left the Garden Tomb in Israel.

Scooting closer to me, she said," Tell me about it."

"Bill has released me to share this horrible story, or I wouldn't tell anyone. He took communion as an unbeliever. He even wants me to write about it!" I watched her face for any reaction, but she stared straight ahead and said nothing. "Eleanor, did you hear me? Bill took communion for all the wrong reasons."

"I heard you."

After I told her everything that had happened in the last two weeks, she sighed heavily and reminded me of Jesus' mercy and grace.

I felt uneasy about what she would say next, so I found myself standing up to take a confrontational stance. "What are you trying to say?" I demanded.

"God didn't love Bill any less after he took communion than He had before. If God could show you love and mercy, Linda, would He do any less for your husband?"

I hung my head with guilt and answered in a soft whisper, "Of course not."

"You had the right motive but a heart full of judgment. You need to re-examine yourself. You're writing a book about being judgmental, and you cast the first stone?"

After she had left, I was in a state of despair. Guilt overwhelmed me and I knew she was right. I had twisted the story to make Bill look bad. But in truth, I was trying to control the situation at the tomb. I wanted Bill to accept Jesus as his personal savior, so I could take the credit and feel valued. I could see me shouting the good news to my friends: "If you pray hard enough and help make a way, your spouse will finally see the light!" God will not share his glory with another, and He doesn't need my help.

I was ashamed of my thoughts, and took ownership of my wrongdoings, by asking Bill for forgiveness, again.

He said, "No apology necessary."

The lessons I learned from Israel are twofold: I don't need to inflict my self-righteous judgments on others, and I'm still an imperfect and unfinished work in process. I still need a lot of practice to get the dance right.

God is not surprised that I fell into self-centeredness, and He loves me too much to let me remain in darkness. The Bible assures me that I am forgiven and helps me to see where I am going and where I have been. II Corinthians 4:6 shows us, "For God, who said, 'Let there be light in the darkness...'" There is no end to His amazing grace.

Amazing Grace

If you seek, you will find the risen Son,
He never lost sight of what needed to be done.
Sin separates us from God and His perfect will,
Does your light shine bright like a city on a hill?

There is no end to His Amazing Grace,
Communion is offered for everyone to taste.
Share in this service in remembrance of Him,
Jesus' light reflecting on me slowly grew dim.

I was nothing more than a hypocrite,
A sinner that fell deep into a dirty pit.
Judging another to a destiny of doom,
Who am I to declare a verdict or assume?

Father forgave me for my decision,
I cast the first stone from hasty intuition.
Jesus covered my sin with His redeeming love,
Glory to Holy Spirit, Christ, and God above.

God gave me the life I had lived, not because I deserved good health, opportunities, and finances, but because of his unmerited favor. It's not about my love for the Father — it's about His love for me.

Each day that I know my Creator intimately is a new day of grace. God protected me over the years with His shield and armor. Yes, I have a lot of dents to prove it.

Everything that I am today is God's handiwork, not my own. The one thing I could never earn is God's grace. (Ephesians 2:8-9) "For by grace you have been saved by faith, and that not of yourselves, it is the gift of God, not of works, lest anyone should boast."

For many years, I hid behind a religious mask. It's not about acting out a role of righteousness but being transformed into His likeness. 1 Samuel 16:7: "The LORD does not look at the things people see. People look at the outward appearance, but the LORD looks at the heart."

We are the poem that God wanted to write. It's time to quit hiding.

The Life We Were Intended to Live

Standing at a distance
A face concealed from light
Hat pressed below the brows
Finding myself lacking
Hands wringing then vanished
Folded across my chest
Under dark garments
Why am I hiding?

Pretending is my game
Alone in a corner
With mask and costume on

84

Silence will keep me safe
Afraid of standing tall
I was ashamed inside
Camouflaging myself
Why am I hiding?

God rescued me from guilt
To break free from the past
Budding with a new soul
Through Christ Jesus His Son
Equipped for kingdom work
I have been set apart
For this time and purpose
No more hiding me.

There is freedom in taking the mask off. I made a conscious decision that I wanted to be real. We grow, learn and process one step at a time. There isn't a single person or place God can't reach. By showing my scars God set the stage for His glorification. Therefore, I am redeemed and healed embracing the dance of life.

THE RELATIONSHIP DANCE
Moving to Deeper Personal Connections

PART TWO

Dancing With Others

After Bill and I married, the extra income from the wedding business gave us opportunities to travel. During that time, I met many people of different cultures, denominations, and beliefs. We are all radically different but have similar desires. Humans want to be loved, to feel valued and worthy. There is a freedom one feels when one is loved without judgment.

In our circle of friends, everyone knew I was a Christian, and they knew that Bill wasn't, but I didn't know much about their religious viewpoints. After much prayer, and talking with Bill, I decided to jump right in and ask if my friends minded sharing their opinions about God. To my surprise, no one turned me down.

Our lives entwine for a reason. As much as some fight it, people need each other. For example, when I fall, my husband and friends pick me up. If I stumble on life's path, they encourage me to stay focused and on course. Still, others help me to be accountable to the community and myself.

The first part of this book revealed that I no longer shuffle along in life on my own, but follow God's path. The second part of this book contains some eye-opening interviews and a few inspirational stories from people whose paths have crossed mine. Part Two is proof that God intervenes in my relationships with others even if they don't put Christ in their lives the same way I do.

So let the dance continue...

Selma

When I first moved to Dalton, I taught dance and gymnastic classes at the National Guard Armory. One day when I was teaching, a woman and a small child poked their heads into the door opening. I stopped the music and walked over to them. "May I help you? I'm right in the middle of a lesson."

"Hi. I'm Selma." Looking to the child at her left side, she said "This is my daughter, Kathy. We're here to observe your classes. Please, go ahead and finish."

I finished my class, and, after I had hugged the children good-bye, Selma pulled Kathy behind her to approach me. She said, "I love to tap dance. I used to be a Radio City Music Hall Rockette in New York City. I would like to get back to dancing again."

I had registered over one hundred students that year, and I couldn't handle all the classes myself, so the first thing that came out of my mouth was, "Do you want a job?"

Selma said, "I would love a job, but first let me see if my husband Wally is okay with that."

The following week, Selma called to let me know that Wally thought taking the job was a splendid idea.

I responded happily, "Great, I will get back with you when we register for our next season."

A few months later, I opened a new studio in a commercial building down the street. Selma would teach classes after I went home in the evenings. We shared the love of dance and the stage for many years. We danced in charity shows to raise money for the local school, and we participated in local theater musicals, providing choreography, and sometimes dancing ourselves. Selma's other love was Jesus. She was definitely a Jesus girl in her actions and testimony. She was the one person in Dalton I would run to if I had questions about being a Christian. I trusted her and shared some of my past mistakes. She never judged me or pointed a finger. I only felt loved and safe.

Selma amazed me with the joy and enthusiasm she had for life. I remember when she started taking Taekwondo lessons. I would go and watch her do a few demonstrations. In her sixties, she became a second-degree black belt in Taekwondo and did a solo at Dalton Trade Center, performing with the South Korean Demonstration Team. Selma and our friend Margaret put together a dance troupe called the Marl-Sel Tap Dancers and performed all over Georgia, winning many senior talent competitions.

Selma was a breast cancer survivor for twenty years, and then, in 2007, found out she had ovarian cancer. She had surgery to remove the cancer followed by chemo treatments. After a year, her high white blood cell count returned, and she resumed treatments. Two years later, a new chemo formula kept her and her family hopeful. *Hope* is a word Christians use often. 1 Peter 1, it tells us, "In God's great mercy He has given us new birth into a living hope through the resurrection of Jesus and our inheritance that can never perish and kept in Heaven." Through our faith we are shielded by God's power, but, for a little, while we will have to endure grief in all kinds of trials.

When the cancer came back the last time, Selma fought hard and suffered much, but I never heard her complain. She and her husband of fifty-five years were strong believers in Christ. If anyone could be called a saint, it would have been Selma. In the thirty-eight years I knew her, she never once spoke bad about another person or judged anyone. She was always there for me, even after I moved seven hours away. Sick as she was fighting cancer, when I visited, she made a way to see me. I was astonished by the love she had for Jesus and for God's will to be done. She is one person that I can say lived out her faith to the end. Selma and I often talked about Heaven. The last conversation we had when she was in the hospital was, "Linda, I'm tired, and I want to go home to see Jesus. I'll be waiting for you."

I asked, "How will I know you, Selma?"

Sounding tired, she said, "Look for the gold tap shoes; I will be the one happily dancing my way toward you."

A few days later, Wally called me and said his precious wife had passed on. She now resides with Jesus.

With time, we learn to live without lost loved ones, but the ache of missing Selma will never disappear.

I dedicate this story to Selma, to the ones who have fought the battle, to the ones who are still fighting, and to all the people who love them. Each day I live, I am one day closer to dancing with her again.

Saying Goodbye

Selma, the dancer, was a friend of mine,
There's a time to leave our loved ones behind.
God's children can't be snatched out of His hand;
She now lives with God in the Promised Land.

My sister lived by faith and not by sight;
A place in Heaven is your new birthright.
Jesus left to prepare a place for you;
Believe in Him is all you had to do.

No more suffering, crying, death, or pain,
Being His, you have everything to gain.
Jesus was sacrificed to be the lamb,
You're now in the arms of the great I Am.

Our Lord died on the cross so we might live,
Through His grace, he taught us how to forgive.
Death has been swallowed up by victory,
Good-bye, dear friend; you are totally free.

Practical Steps

Dancing is the physical awareness that comes from the joy within us.

Reese

Reese and I were both young mothers in our 30s when she brought her daughters to my dance studio in 1987. I found out she owned a hair salon, and I booked an appointment. After that first cut-and-color, I became a regular customer, and we met weekly to talk about our professional successes and our personal lives. She quickly became my emotional supporter.

Fifteen years later, I was a single mom, and Reese was raising her daughter's little girl. Raising children and running businesses got in the way, but we still tried to have a girl date now and then. She is the kind of friend that even though you don't talk for months, when you do get together, it's like you were never apart.

After I moved to Alabama, and both of us were in our fifties, we tried to stay connected.

Recently, I called Reese to tell her I was staying at the campgrounds and would like to visit. She said, "You know what? You are always coming to Dalton to visit me. Let me come to your RV site in Chatsworth. I always wanted to check out where you parked your home away from home."

"That would be great, Reese. I'll text the directions."

I was pleased she was going to make the effort, so I tidied our 'palace on wheels' and fixed us a light lunch.

Reese arrived, and we caught up with each other's lives. To my surprise, she told me that she and Clay had received custody of his two-year-old grandson. We agreed that being friends helps us be more prepared to deal with life's surprises.

Over lunch, I asked her if I could tell of our friendship in my book. She didn't hesitate to say, "Sure."

"Let's begin with some history together," I said.

Reese told me a few things I didn't remember. I laughed out loud when she refreshed my memory about the day she asked me over to help redecorate her house many years earlier—soon after we met. We started in her bedroom. I took one glance around and told her she needed to remove her vacation mementos. She said quickly, "Those trinkets happen to be reminders of the good times I have had and I don't want to remove them."

I said, "Okay, let's move on to the girls' bedroom."

We walked down the hall, and Reese turned on the light to their room. I looked around and muttered, "It would make the room look bigger if you separated their personal items." Reese was not happy with my comments.

I quickly grabbed her arm and said, "Let's go downstairs to the den," but when we got there, I blurted out, "It's cold and dark down here." Reese turned on the lights, with a frown on her face. I mumbled, "If we don't stop this quest to decorate your home, we might get into a cat fight."

She agreed and said, "Let's call it a day."

Since Reese helped me through my third divorce, I asked her what came to mind about my abusive relationship with Lee.

She said, "Before you married Lee, I told you about all the red flags I saw. I could name each one because I had been in an abusive marriage myself."

"I do remember you saying something about that, but I chose not to listen. Proverbs 19:20 tells us, 'Listen to advice and accept discipline, and at the end you will be counted among the wise.' I wasn't wise, was I?"

Reese took another bite of salad. To break the silence, she asked, "Do you remember the night we went to Lakeshore with our husbands?"

I replied, "No. Go on. I tend to forget a few details of those awful times."

Reese continued, "Lee started picking a fight with you on our way back from Chattanooga. You got quiet and looked like a puppy that had been kicked. I couldn't stand it any longer and told Lee I didn't appreciate the way he was talking to you. I said, 'Linda is a small woman. If you want to pick a fight with a woman your size, fight with me.' Tim stopped the car, and I told Lee to get out."

"Then what?" I asked.

"I told you that I was taking you home with us and that we should let Lee get back the best way he could. You needed a safe place to go, and he needed to sleep his anger off. You were nervous but, between sobs, you agreed. You paced the bedroom floor all night, and the next morning you wanted to go home. I couldn't talk you out of it so; I drove you back to your house. We went inside, and Lee was gone. Most of your furniture was smashed to pieces. You called the police to make a report. When the police arrived, you told me to leave and you were going to pack a few things and stay at another friend's house for a few days so you could think."

I cleared our plates and asked Reese if she wanted more tea.

She said, "Yes." After I returned to the table our conversation turned to Christianity. Reese said, "I am a good person, but have left Jesus out of my life. I'm not where I need to be."

I asked Reese, "Do you feel uncomfortable talking about religion and your relationship with God?"

She replied, "No. I just don't talk about it with many people, including my children. You know I believe in a higher being, but I'm not in church. I guess you would call me a dysfunctional believer."

Smiling at Reese to break the tension I said, "I like how you said *dysfunctional believer*."

She said, "I can't believe I came up with that!"

When I asked her about Jesus, she said, "He is the Son of God. Remember you gave me the verses several years ago when we were sitting on the steps at your condo."

"Yes. Refresh my memory about that particular day. Did you accept Jesus?"

"Linda, I have always been saved, but I guess I rededicated my life that day. As you know, neither of us was attending church and putting God first in our lives."

I said, "I know very well. Who do you say Jesus was?"

"He made a way for the unchosen people to be chosen. The Gentiles were not the selected people, right?"

I wasn't sure how to answer her, so I replied, "Do you think you're chosen, Reese?"

She said, "I'm not sure."

I replied, "For me, I don't think much about if I'm chosen or not. What's important to me is that I'm in a relationship with God, and I have a passion for pleasing Him. Let's drop it and move on. Do you pray?"

"Not really. I don't have a desire to pray," she replied, shrugging her shoulders.

Our conversation ended rather abruptly as we both glanced at the outdoor clock hanging on the RV. I said, "Didn't you say earlier you had to leave at 2:00 to meet your client for a hair appointment?" She nodded yes.

After she left, I knew it wouldn't be long before I started missing her. The main thing we have always had in common is that we are each other's burden bearers. There is a verse in Hebrews 10:25: "Not giving up meeting together, as some are in the habit of doing, but encouraging one another and all the more as you see the day approaching." Reese has been in my life for many years. She continues to help carry my burdens and to delight in my joy. What a treasure to have a lifelong friend!

Practical Steps

History builds stepping stones for the future.

liv

Darla

Darla was born in England where she met her childhood sweetheart, Doug. Darla and Doug came to American holding green cards in 1991. They loved America and the opportunities it offered. They found their way to Atlanta where Darla sold real estate, and Doug worked in construction. It might be easy to look at their lives and think they have it made with several homes, a thriving business, boats, a private plane, and many friends, but their good fortune followed hard work and well-laid plans.

A couple of years after they arrived in the States, Doug received a job overseeing a marina on a lake in eastern Tennessee. After the marina went into foreclosure a few years later, the owners asked Doug if he and Darla would like to negotiate a deal to take over the property. They took the challenge.

They lived over the marina office for years, managing their enterprise and being on call 24-7 during the summer months. They have weathered several storms that have destroyed the marina, but have stayed committed to making a success of their business and helping customers have fun on the lake.

I met Doug and Darla because Bill had a houseboat at their marina, and he had been friends with them since 2000. When Bill introduced us, they were glad to finally see him happy and enjoying a companion who loved the water as much as he did. They accepted me as part of the boating community and were guests at our wedding.

Over the years, we have stayed in contact even though we lived in different states. One evening, Darla called and said, "Guess what? Doug and I are both US citizens!"

I replied, "That's great news! I can't wait to tell Bill."

I assumed it was important to her to let us know the news. After we hung up the phone, I felt our relationship took a turn toward a deeper friendship.

We see each other as often as we can, but it is challenging because of their work hours. Darla and I enjoy taking early morning walks together and talking about everyday life. In the thirteen years I have known the Kyles, Darla had never brought up her feelings about God until I mentioned I was writing a book about how friends can build relationships even if they don't have the same beliefs about religion. I never held back about my faith, but, to be honest, I was hesitant to ask about hers. One day she said," You never asked to interview me." That was a door I was going to swing open.

I said, "Do you have time to answer a few questions as we walk?"

"I do."

"Tell me about your upbringing in England," I said.

Darla said, "My mom and my siblings and I attended church and Sunday school when I was a child."

"What about your dad?"

"He only went on Christmas, Easter, and special occasions. Religion wasn't talked about in our home. Our culture was "actions speak louder than words." Americans talk about things like love and God, but my family didn't. My parents never said *I love you* in words, but my brother and sisters knew they loved us."

I replied, "So, the church was an action step?"

"Yes. When I turned fifteen, I got to choose to go to church or stop," she replied.

"What did you decide?" I asked.

"I stopped attending church and started living by the Golden Rule. The principles of *don't kill, don't steal.* You know—the Ten Commandments. I'm not an evil person."

"Define an evil person."

"They are the ones who do the unspeakable and have no remorse."

"Who is God to you?" I asked.

"I do believe in God, but I don't have to go to church—just follow the Ten Commandments. As I got older, I started to think the church was made by humans with personal rules. I'm grateful I was brought up in the church, and the principles you learn there help you to raise a child better."

"What about Jesus?"

Darla said, "He is a fictional character. I mean, he is not God's son, but he teaches us how to live."

"What do you think happens after you take your final breath?"

"I don't know. I would like the luxury to explore the possibilities of seeing my deceased dad again."

I asked Darla if she had any questions. She shook her head no. The next thirty minutes I walked beside my friend in silence before we left in different directions.

Practical Steps

My favorite quote from Albert Camus:
Don't walk in front of me...I may not follow
Don't walk behind me...I may not lead
Walk beside me....Just be my friend

Jackie

For as long as I can remember I have loved the myth of mermaids, and those who visit our home will see many images of them.

During the spring of 2004, while looking for an artist in Baldwin County to paint a few of these beautiful creatures on two of our Adirondack chairs, I entered a local art shop and asked the saleswoman if she knew of a painter who specialized in mermaids.

She said, "Yes. Let me call Jacqueline Falkner and see if she is available." Afterward, the owner gave me a quote to paint the chairs.

I told her, "The price sounds fair! I will be back tomorrow and drop off the chairs."

A few days later, while shopping at a furniture store in town, a spunky, mature lady asked, "Can I help you?"

I asked whether she had any pieces featuring mermaids. She smiled, "Are you a mermaid enthusiast?"

Nodding, I said, "I sure am!"

"I know another lady in town who likes mermaids."

Curious, I asked, "Who?"

"I think her name is Linda Center."

With my mouth hanging open and pointing to myself, I exclaimed, "That's me! How do you know that?"

She said with a broad grin, "My name is Jackie Falkner, short for Jacqueline, and I'm the lady who is painting your Adirondack chairs. I'm filling in for the owner here. I dropped by an hour ago to bring a few paintings, and my friend, the proprietress, asked me to mind the store."

That is how I met this fascinating, artistic woman with dark auburn hair and a love for mermaids.

Afterwards, I retained her services for a few art projects. Her efforts and talents put extra touches of love in our home. Jackie took a real interest in making our home feel special with nautical mosaic tile, stained glass, and painted mermaids in the bathrooms. During breaks, we talked about her former dance studios and world travels. We shared a lot in common, and our business agreement turned into a friendship.

Jackie and her husband, Larry, are interesting people. They sold everything they owned and traveled on their sailboat all over the world for three years. Afterward, they sold the sailboat but continued to travel. My husband and I accompanied them on a cruise to Panama and another time met them in Barcelona, Spain.

For the decade from 2004 through 2014, Jackie was busy teaching dance and art classes. When her schedule allowed, she and her husband traveled or spent time with family. I noticed they never talked about God or attending church. That didn't stop me talking about what God was doing in my life, and she appeared interested. When I asked about her beliefs, she would say, "I don't believe like you do."

I had just begun to outline and draft this book when I thought of Jackie, thinking she would be an ideal person to interview and hoping she might open up a little about her religious preferences. I bit my lip over lunch one day and just blurted out,"Do you believe in God?" Quickly, I squeezed my eyes shut, shocking myself by my bluntness.

To my surprise, Jackie replied, "No one has ever asked my opinion about God. I would like to answer your question because I wrote a letter recently to my grandchildren on that very subject."

From previous conversations, I knew Jackie's daughter and family were Christians. Reaching into my purse, I asked her permission to write a few notes while we talked. She nodded. Closing my pocketbook, I looked up to find her blinking, trying to hold back tears. She began, "After visiting my granddaughter a few months back she sat on my lap, patted my face and told me, 'Grandma, I will miss you when you die because momma told me you were going down there since you don't believe in Jesus.'"

Jackie was beside herself with the words from an innocent child. I thought to myself that nothing works as it should in relationships if we are not careful with our words. It made me wonder how many times I wasn't sensitive to the words I said to others. Judging and condemning people to Hell is not the way to win people to Christ.

We had spoken of our past during our time together, and I knew Jacqueline's parents were divorced. She added additional background information as she explained, "My mother was unsociable, and my father was an alcoholic."

"What about your background concerning God?" I quietly asked.

Jackie answered, "As far as religion goes, I call God the Creator. He can be called many things by many humans that fit their lives. I think the rules He laid down for us are perhaps different than what He provided for others thousands of years ago or for the future. Our needs are different at various times. I think organized religions were created by mankind and are flawed. Each one has some bad ideas slipped in by man, but God trusts us to be wise enough to see those flaws. The Creator gave each of us a soul. We had a need from the beginning of time to fill that soul with a god, whether it is Buddha, Mohammad, nature, or God in Heaven. I pray all the time. We could be talking to our conscious from our sub-conscious. I think God gave us the instructions regarding saying grace and praying so we would build a habit of talking to Him often. For families, it is vital to help children develop the habit of prayer. I know this is right for me because He answers my prayers. Whenever I cannot hear Him, I take a hard look at my life and usually find I have wandered from the path He has chosen for me to walk. He is not failing to answer; I have just wandered too far away to hear His gentle voice."

I picked up on her words—grace, prayer path, gentle voice. Therefore, I could hardly wait to ask her the next question. "Do you believe in the Bible?"

She answered, "I do not believe the Bible in a word-for-word sense. I know most Christians believe very strongly about studying and understanding every word. That is right for them and perhaps for you. I feel the Bible was written under God's inspiration, but through men of long ago. They had less knowledge than we do now. There are examples where I think things were stated in a way that people at that time needed certain rules to live by that we no longer need. Man included many things in the Bible that were not inspired by God. I believe that early in our history, men changed some of the Bible to suit the Church's control over the populace. I feel God gave us all the intelligence to judge what are the useful and significant lessons which help humankind thrive. It is my belief that all His standards taught by Jesus and elsewhere in the Bible are simply the same rules needed to live in a civilized society. It matters not, whether you learn them from the Bible or from the God-given wisdom we all have."

"What are your feelings about church, Jackie?" I asked.

"I think church is very important to most people, and a wonderful place to learn and grow as a Christian. Most people are social, they thrive by being in groups, and I assume most people get more from worship as a group. People like being in a building they feel is dedicated to worship and seem to feel 'closer' to God in church. Most Christians need the support of each other and to praise the Lord together. I have never felt God's presence in church. All I feel is surrounded by people enclosed in a building built by men. Since modern-day church services are based on studying the Bible word-for-word, the sermons are seldom relevant to me. Instead, I feel God's presence when I am outdoors, in the woods, on the water, at the beach, anywhere created by Him, not man. I feel Him when we are alone, He and I. I feel Him when I am awed by the beauty and wonder He created, by the soul He gave me with the ability to appreciate that beauty and wonder. I know people say that is just a pretty, poetic way to excuse myself from attending church…and for years I believed that and felt guilty. Finally, I got old enough to realize I would be attending church if it were relevant to me. I would not, instead, feel the daily need to be alone in nature to talk to Him and to be quiet enough to hear His answers. That tells me this is the relationship He wants with me. I think we must each find the place we feel God's presence and should meet him there, often."

"I agree Jackie. Are you okay? Is there anything else you want to discuss?"

"I'm good. Are we done?"

"Yes, Ma'am."

After we said our goodbyes, I kept thinking about the letter Jackie wrote to her grandchildren. *Good for her*, I thought. It's a great idea to share our beliefs with others. If their thoughts are different, let God intervene. When my grandchildren become adults they will find their own answers and hopefully find peace.

Practical Steps

We must watch our words. The tongue has the power of life and death.

Mary

Heat radiated through the windshield, and I could feel the sun warm my upturned face as I drove down a small county road. I turned on the radio, and my body automatically swayed to the music. I was driving to Fairhope, Alabama, to visit with my heart daughter.

In my experiences with my inner circle of friends, I have found there are people I meet for a reason—maybe a shared purpose. I would call these people casual acquaintances. I find unity with others for a season—maybe for a few years or many. But somehow, for some reason, we separate and move on with life with different interests. The valuable friendships reconnect as we share the milestones. I can count on these few friends in the valleys, and we celebrate mountain top-experiences together. Sharing peak experiences reduces the depths of the valleys.

You know the old quote from Harper Lee: You can choose your friends but you sho' can't choose your family.

From 2005 through 2012, I volunteered as a counselor at a local pregnancy center. My first client was Mary. She was in her early twenties, and she had come in for a pregnancy test. I could tell she was nervous. Taking her into a private room to ask a few questions, I learned she was unmarried and frightened of childbirth.

Informing Mary that her test was indeed positive, I held her as she cried and could hear her gasp for breath. After she had relaxed, I asked her to come back and take the six-week parenting classes the center offered. I told her that if she attended all classes and completed her homework, she would be rewarded with a complete layette for her newborn. She agreed, and we began to bond.

Before she left, we held hands, and I asked her if I could pray for her. She hesitated, so I said, "Prayers open the door for God to work in our lives."

Mary stiffened and whispered, "Okay." Afterward, she smoothed her hair and gathered her purse, and we walked out to the reception area to book her first parenting class appointment.

A few weeks later Mary came to class, and we talked. I told her it takes strength of will for an unmarried woman to decide to put up with the whispers, looks, and pointed fingers for the sake of her child. I told her she could cope with it all once she understood that God wanted His best for her, and that He cared for her and the baby she was carrying. Jesus died so we could be adopted into the family of God. Mary listened to my words, and made the choice to follow Christ. While crying and smiling at the same time, I realized in that defining moment, I saw Mary as my heart daughter.

Each time we met, Mary was excited to share what the Lord was doing in her life. She became less fearful, and one could easily see her growing in the strength of our Lord. After our last session together, I told Mary I would visit her in the hospital as our student-teacher relationship had turned into one of trust and warmth.

The next week, I found a note in my Bible from Mary. In it, she told me how much her experience at the center had helped her and provided the support she had so desperately needed.

The day she called to say her baby was born, I couldn't get to the hospital fast enough! Holding her beautiful baby daughter, Mia, in my arms brought such joy. God not only gave Mary a precious gift, but He gave me one.

Driving from the hospital, I was overwhelmed with joy for Mary and myself. It reminded me of a Bible verse, "Be joyful always." (Phil 3:1). Joy is a little word but the initials represent a big statement: Jesus On You. Our goal as Christ-followers is to become a living expression of joy every day. When we savor the simple pleasures of life, it lifts our joy level up a notch.

Over the years, Mary, Mia, and I have made many memories—birthdays, summer fun outings, and church services. Mary and I take the time to invest in our relationship. When I get to missing my out-of-state children, Mary fills the hole in my heart.

Sitting outside at lunch recently, we were both giggling like school children. I told her it was good to laugh, and it made me happy to see her take her role as a mother seriously.

I couldn't help but wonder if Mary and Mia's father, Sammy, would ever marry. Since Mia's birth, Sammy has been involved in their lives. He comes around occasionally and offers financial support. Their income is limited since Mary chooses to be a stay-at-home mother.

I shook the thoughts from my head as Mary shared more about herself as a child. "My father was never around, and our mother knew about God but never knew Him personally. I remember a nice lady named Alice, with a family of her own, who drove thirty miles to pick up my siblings and me to take us to church, and then we would go to her home for lunch." Alice made a permanent impression on Mary. It seemed like a natural friendship involving loving and being loved.

Mary added that her mother is deaf and cannot talk. There was a pained stare in her eyes when she added, "I believe that in Heaven I will hear my mother's voice for the first time."

Heading home, I thought about the last thing Mary told me about her mother's impairment. In God's great love and wisdom, He has created Heaven as a place of perfect peace, health, and happiness. I like to think what a day of rejoicing it will be when Mary can hear her mother's voice.

Practical Steps

Nurture your friendships; they are the family you get to choose.

Carla

Studying the Bible with other women brings me joy. My church launched a women's study group, and I volunteered to lead the class. Carla Johnson, a snowbird from Wisconsin, first came to one of my Bible study sessions in 2013. Every Sunday, Carla would attend, hungry for the infallible Word of God. Following each lesson, we had a sharing time. Carla was quiet during these sessions, and, if I asked her a direct question, she would exclaim she needed to process it before she could answer. She told me later after one of our sessions, "Linda, I feel the other ladies know more about the Bible than I do."

"That's okay. Everyone starts somewhere, and you have made the first step, just coming to Bible study. Please keep attending. You won't regret it."

Carla is kindhearted. She makes cookies and beaded jewelry to give to others. I had seen her knit prayer shawls in church and discovered that she gives them away to anyone who needs a soft, warm touch. She is a unique pearl in my circle of treasured friends. As with women in the Bible, I have seen God turn Carla's shyness into a mighty boldness in what the Lord is doing in her life and family.

Carla and I attended a Christian Women's conference April, 2015, in Pensacola. We got to spend several hours developing a deeper relationship. I learned she was a cancer survivor. Ten years earlier, during an annual physical, her doctor suspected breast cancer. After the diagnosis, she had two surgeries—first a lumpectomy in her right breast, and then, two weeks later, they removed edges of the cancer that remained. The surgeries were followed by six weeks of radiation, during which she lost all her hair. Carla told me when she glances at her chest, the scars left on her body remind her that faith helped carry her through her ordeal.

After the conference, Carla and her husband of twenty-five happy years, Terry, returned to their northern home in the spring. When they arrived in Wisconsin in May, Carla scheduled her annual check-up.

At the radiologist's office, Carla and Terry received the shocking results that cancer had returned in the same breast and a mastectomy was recommended. Leaving the office, they both were thinking, "How could this happen again?" Having fought cancer before, she knew she had a rough journey ahead of her.

I called Carla several times to check on her and see how she was doing. She had a positive attitude and would say God's presence and protection were with her every step of the way.

The mastectomy was followed by reconstructive surgery two months later. Healing was swift and without complications. She had supernatural strength and peace to cope with these challenges.

She was in the hands of skilled surgeons, a nurse navigator, and the best caregiver in the world—her husband. Carla's face would beam, telling me how Terry cleaned her bandages, reminded her to take all medications, and drove her to doctor appointments.

Carla doesn't think of her cancer as a setback, but as a wellness journey. She felt wrapped in prayers and has developed a deeper love and trust in God. Carla is blessed to be a cancer survivor once again. She is brand new and ready to start over. She is an inspiration to all that have or will ever have cancer. The God Carla knows, cares about every detail of her life. Jesus tells us every hair on our heads is counted.

She has recovered well from her surgeries. Carla did not have radiation this time or chemo, so her hair remained intact.

When Carla and her husband returned to Gulf Shores in the fall of 2015, I asked her if I could share her cancer journey to help others that might be struggling with this horrible disease. She was eager to pass on what she has learned, physically and spiritually.

God takes us on different paths to bring us closer to him and never gives us more than we can bear. Carla tells everyone, " I have found there's a new day coming, and joy will eventually return."

That reminds me of a scripture in Psalm 30:11 "You turned my wailing into dancing; you removed my sackcloth and covered me with joy."

Edgar Allan Poe said, "Never to suffer would never to have been blessed." I have endured pain through love and loss, and the blessings of getting to the other side outweigh the suffering. The misery prepared me for ministry.

Practical Steps

Your personal story could encourage hope for others.

Connie

Connie Simon travels to Gulf Shores and surrounding areas performing marriage ceremonies. We first talked in 2006, when I inquired about her services as a minister for a wedding I was coordinating. I found Reverend Connie friendly and educated, and she was available for the date I needed.

The day of the wedding, Connie showed up early, professionally dressed in a black robe, carrying a Bible, and wearing a cross around her neck. Her husband, John, escorted her since Connie doesn't drive. She has a way about her that instantly allows everyone around her to feel comfortable.

Connie was a big encourager in my life. She attended several Christian events where I was the guest speaker. Afterwards, she would comment about what she observed. Connie was an unconventional minister. I liked that, and so did my clients who requested a non-denominational officiant.

Connie talked about the Lord and how blessed she was, but I didn't know details about her life. We started talking about her youth. Connie said, "My parents liked to party a lot. During the week, they boarded me at a nearby farm. Mother would pick me up on Fridays, after work. She took me to church on Sunday mornings and returned me to the farm every Sunday night."

Interrupting her, I asked if she had good memories of the farm and the couple who acted as her surrogate parents during the week.

She replied, "They weren't nice people."

I asked if she was abused.

Looking down, she said, "Yes." I dropped the subject, feeling sick inside.

"Did your father attend church with you?"

She said, "Never! He believed he was God. My father resented my mother going to church because his meals would be delayed. There was a lot of physical abuse in our home. That is one reason I married at eighteen—to get out of the house."

"Tell me about your marriage."

Connie began, "I got married in the Catholic Church, and the marriage lasted ten years. During that marriage, I started to work as a singer. I got pregnant, but lost my little boy to crib death. While separated from my husband and God, I worked as a secretary in Washington, D.C. After a year, I moved back to Massachusetts, and I met John, my present husband, at a dance club. We dated a few years and married in 1973. After my son was born, I wanted to understand the Bible, find God, and pursue my spiritual beliefs."

I asked her to explain.

She said, "I studied and practiced levitation, healing, and performed as a medium. I received my degree and was ordained in 1983 with Tzaddi. I obtained my doctorate in 1987."

I was not familiar with the Tzaddi worship, so I looked it up after our interview. Tzaddi religion is based on developing spiritually. Followers rejoice in the divine toward others, nature, and in the world.

Connie desires to foster a spiritual community. With that passion in her heart, she opened her chapel in 1999 in Taylor, Texas. Later, in 2003, she and John moved to Alabama and formed another church. I was surprised to hear how much Connie had accomplished in her life. I wanted to ask her more.

"Describe God."

Connie answered, "God is present everywhere at the same time. He is within us."

"Who is Jesus?"

She said, "The Son of God. He is our Savior."

"Do you pray or talk to God?" I asked.

"I settle myself down and meditate. I ask for His forgiveness and thank Him for my gifts. I don't pray at a regular time; usually it's spontaneous."

"Do you believe in the Bible?"

"I do question a few things in the Bible because it contradicts itself. Without the Bible, we would be like animals. The Bible is God's Word, but man has changed it."

My last question was, "Where do you think you go when you take your last breath?"

Connie explained, "I'm not afraid to die. Our loved ones who have passed on come to take us to Heaven. I don't believe in a burning hell. I think we could be living in Hell now."

God's original design was a perfect place and perfect relationships. The promise of Heaven will be life with God and other Christians in an ideal setting. Connie and I both cling to the same hope of Heaven.

Practical Steps

Some friends are a right fit from the start.

Karen

Karen King met with me at International House of Pancakes in Foley in, April, 2011, to invite me to join the board of Southern Women of God. Our spirits connected quickly as we took our first sip of coffee and started chatting. Four weeks later, I was sworn in. Our relationship grew much deeper than just being fellow board members. It became a friendship where we cared for and nurtured each other.

Karen was respected by her peers. She studied the Bible for many years, searching scriptures for guidance in her life. She is gifted in quoting scripture and knows the meaning behind the words. She freely provides wise counsel and prayer. I identify her as my teacher, confidant, and prayer warrior. One day, in her office, she told me her powerful story.

Both of Karen's parents were teachers, and she was an only child. She lived in a rural community and her parents took her to church for social occasions. One Sunday, a fire-and-brimstone preacher came to give the message. After hearing the sermon, she wanted to walk down the aisle and pray to receive God because she was terrified she would die and go to hell. Something stopped her. She was afraid to go down the aisle by herself so she remained seated. Karen told me, "That was my first image of God, and He frightened me."

I mulled over her comment. Karen was a child of nine. Was it God who frightened her or her parents? Maybe it was the preacher. I didn't stop to ask. After Karen graduated from high school and was out from under her parents' influence, she began looking for a new church and found one she liked.

Having a conversation with the youth pastor one day she asked, "I really want to know God. How can I do this?"

The young pastor answered, "You come from a good family. Keep the Ten Commandments, and you will be fine." It's sad to think that no one in Karen's family or leaders in the church ever stopped to show her in the Bible how to meet the Living God. After their conversation, she was confused and depressed. She also felt abandoned by her parents. Wanting to end her loneliness; she swallowed a bottle of aspirin. Thirty minutes later lying on her bed, everything came back up. She cried the rest of the night, thinking she was worthless.

A month later, Karen moved away to college, but she didn't care about anything. She felt isolated, making her very vulnerable. She became heavily involved in paranormal and psychic activities that gave her purpose. At a party, she experienced a date rape. There was no one to tell or any safe place to go. Dealing with the reality of the rape, she believed she didn't matter to any one—especially God—and she turned her back on Him.

Later, when she was in graduate school, she had a car accident and went to the courthouse to pay her fine. There, she met Barry who became her husband six months later. After a few years of physical and verbal abuse, they knew they had made a mistake and separated. Soon, Barry talked Karen into giving their marriage another chance. She said yes, but soon regretted her decision to go back. She felt trapped and unloved, so she had an affair. At age twenty-five, she was diagnosed with clinical depression. She considered suicide because she felt alone, used, and empty. Barry came home one night, and Karen told him everything she had done to hurt herself and others. To her surprise, Barry began to cry and asked her forgiveness for not being there to recognize her pain.

Both of them surrendered their will to God that night and gave their marriage to Him. They had no doubt God heard them, saw their hearts, and saved them. They soon noticed a transformation in each other and in their marriage. Barry studied to obtain his ministry degree; together they started a church in a bar. They shepherded several churches over the years and ended up concentrating on missions. Today they are happily married, retired and waiting for God's next assignment.

I asked Karen what she thought her next assignment might be.

She said, "Many years ago, God brought me to the truth by His Word. Everything I do is based on scriptures. If something doesn't line up with the Word, then it is from man and not God. Psalm 119:105 says, 'Your word is a lamp to guide my feet and a light for my path.'"

"Anything else you want to share before I leave?"

"Yes, there is another thing I want to tell you about my past. I had a near-death experience in 1988. After a cardiac arrest at the age of forty-five, I left my body and was escorted by an angel to Heaven and then to Hell."

"I have heard of people having out-of-body experiences, but let's save this story for our next visit," I said. Tilting my head to the side I explained, "I must get home to fix dinner and don't want to be rushed. Can we get together soon?"

"Of course," Karen replied.

God had a protective hand over Karen's life. He loved her even when she turned her back on Him. Karen received Christ's intervention in her life with renewed strength and purpose. She once was guilty but now liberated simply by surrendering her will to God and acknowledging she was a sinner. God filled the void in Karen and Barry's life and relationship.

Practical Steps

Meeting Jesus, right where you are changes hearts and changes lives.

Patricia

Four years ago, our mutual love of gardening brought Patricia Lyles into my life. I remember chatting with her at our local garden club meeting. After the meeting was over, I asked Patricia if she would like to join me for lunch.

"I would enjoy that!" she exclaimed.

During lunch, we discussed middle age, marriages, family, and hobbies. We found out both of us enjoyed kayaking, riding bikes, and playing cards.

A few weeks later we decided to get together to ride bikes. On our outing, I shared what God was doing in my life. Patricia made it clear that she didn't believe in God or religion. However, that didn't stop me from enjoying her company and friendship. Patricia has always respected me and my love for the Lord. One day after kayaking, her hip was bothering her. I asked if I could pray. She explained, "I don't have faith in prayer."

I smiled and whispered, "I have enough faith for both of us." I put my hand on her hip, and she allowed me to pray. There was another instance when I was speaking at a women's gathering at Gulf Shores United Methodist Church. I begged Patricia to come. She whined, "I haven't been to church in years," but she wanted to support me, so she agreed to the invitation.

Patricia knew I had the joy of the Lord in my life and depended on Him. She never once told me not to talk about God. One day I had an opportunity to ask Patricia about her childhood. I watched my words carefully as I asked Patricia to open up about her past and her beliefs about the church, the Bible, and God.

She replied, "I have no problem talking about that. I come from a Catholic background but was never confirmed. I remember attending a Catholic school while in second or third grade, living in California. I was the middle of five children. My parents would drop us off for mass; they gave us ten cents each to put in the collection plate. Instead of putting the money in the offering, we walked to McDonald's after mass and bought fries.

I grabbed my friend's arm and said, "You're kidding!"

After both of us stopped laughing, Patricia said, "Can you believe fries cost ten cents back in the fifties?"

"I married Danny forty-nine years ago in the Lutheran church. My parents weren't happy about it, but they attended the wedding. Five years later, we had a wedding ceremony in a Catholic church. That's my history. Now you can start with the questions."

"How would you describe God?"

She answered, "I have no description. I don't believe in God."

"Have you ever talked to a supernatural being or thing when you were in need?"

She answered, "I did at one time when I needed help. I don't do that anymore. I help myself. I don't give thanks to anything or anyone."

"Who do you think Jesus was?"

"He was a good man. I don't believe in God, so I don't believe Jesus was God's son. I definitely don't believe Jesus was resurrected."

"What do you think of the Bible?"

"Stories like Adam & Eve, Noah, Moses—they are all fiction. The miracles in the Bible credited to what Jesus did, he didn't do."

"What do you think happens after death?"

"My body decays, and I will be part of the earth again."

Patricia's soul and mind were empty of anything that pertained to God. Lost for words, I stared at her with a heavy feeling in my stomach.

Patricia said, "I get it; you want me to go where you think you go for eternity."

Stumbling for the right words, I knew this was a critical point that might destroy our relationship or bring harmony. I remember reading Psalm 141 in which David prayed, "Set a guard over my mouth, Lord; keep watch over the door of my lips." This moment with Patricia was an open door for an opportunity to show Jesus' love. I didn't want to slam it shut, so I put a smile on my face and hugged my friend goodbye and said, "Let's get together tomorrow for lunch."

"Where and when?" She asked.

"How about Sierra's around one o'clock?"

Patricia arrived first and was sitting by a window waiting for me. The first thing she said as I sat down was, "What have you been doing this morning?"

I told her, "I have been at a women's retreat. The gathering was about God's Design." I asked her, "Have I ever shared how I came to know Christ?"

She said, "No, but I'm interested."

After I had given my testimony, she started asking me questions. For once I thought I saw a flicker of light in her eyes and felt positive that she might want to know more about Jesus. I was hopeful that God was making a way to reveal himself to her. We chatted some more and finished our lunch. Right before I left, I said, "Patricia, if I'm wrong about Jesus, I have nothing to lose, but if you are wrong, what will you lose?"

She shook her head and corrected me, "Sorry. I have nothing to lose!"

I bit my tongue.

We paid our bill, and on the way out of the restaurant, I kindly said, "Love you, girlfriend."

She said, "Love you, too. We will get together soon."

Patricia and I value each other's company. The need to be right can destroy friendships, but humility promotes unity.

Practical Steps

Our lives are better when we share a dance than if we never dance at all.

The Williams

A friend of mine mentioned she had dinner with friends who were leaving on a cruise to Spain the next day. As my husband, Bill, and I were also booked on the same cruise, Brenda thought we might like to meet them, so she gave me their contact information. The next day, I called Ruth and Charles Williams.

"Hello, Ruth. We have never met, but we have a mutual friend! My name is Linda Center, and I live down the street. Brenda Frazier gave me your number. Are you taking the cruise out of Tampa Bay to Barcelona?"

"Yes, we are! In fact, we're on our way to Tampa, as we speak," Ruth replied.

"Would you like to meet?" I asked.

"Yes, that would be fun!" she said.

Driving to the cruise terminal, I told Bill, "Let's meet for dinner. If they are boring, we can excuse ourselves."

Guess what? The Williams had the same thought!

The first evening on the ship, we met for dinner. Charles was a tall man with twinkling eyes behind bronze frame glasses. Ruth was an attractive brunette and full of life. We enjoyed each other's company. They were not boring, and we found that we had a lot in common. Like us, they had brought children and careers from previous marriages into their union. Ruth and Charles enjoy spending time with their grandchildren, and it's obvious their family is the joy of their lives. They like to travel, and we became friends instantly.

Returning home, we kept in contact. Many times, I shared my love for Jesus with Ruth and Charles but I wasn't sure of their beliefs or faith. If problems or illness attacked their family they would ask for prayer, so I knew they believed in God.

A year later, Charles and Ruth visited us at Standing Rock RV Resort in North Georgia, where we have a vacation lot. Ruth called a week later. She said, "Are you sitting down? This morning we received word that they accepted our bid on a lot and RV just down the road from yours!"

One day I asked if I could pick on them for the purpose of my book. Both looked at each other, and Charles said, "Sure, why not?" We chose a date for the following week at the campgrounds.

The day of the interview, I woke up to a beautiful, peaceful morning. One morning while Bill busied himself cleaning up our lot in preparation for leaving town, I walked to Ruth and Charles' RV, with pen and paper in hand. I stepped onto their wooden porch and was greeted with smiles and fresh coffee. As I sat down, I was excited to interview them and get to know their family connections. Charles went first.

"What kind of background do you want?" he answered with a smirk.

I asked, "Were you brought up in a Christian home?"

Charles explained, "My folks were believers and attended church. I remember seeing my parents read the Bible, and my father highlighted and underlined scriptures in his Bible. My parents prayed together." He turned to his wife and said, "Your turn."

Ruth began, "My parents took my brother and me to church, but they didn't go. They never talked about God or religion. My mother told me that she found God in her later years. Personally, I had a bad experience in the church. The people that attended told me I was going to hell and I was a hypocrite for some of my choices in life."

I thought to myself, 'I understand why Ruth has a bad taste for Christians in her mouth.' But I didn't comment and went to the next question. "How would you describe God?"

Charles spoke first. "I'm pretty much agnostic. We are not here by accident. I can see God in nature, birds, and trees." He paused and then continued, "Linda, life is random. God doesn't control us. I don't believe we are preordained or predestined. We have free will and should take care of ourselves. If something bad happens, it's because you were at the wrong place at the wrong time."

Ruth spoke up, "God created this Earth. I do believe in God. We control a lot of what happens to us. If an opportunity arises, we need to go with it. We have God within us!"

"Who do you think Jesus is?"

Charles, looking me straight in the eyes, answered, "Jesus was a great historical figure. I don't believe he was the son of God. This man was intelligent and charismatic. He came from nowhere and created a following. His finest teaching was to love one another."

Ruth agreed with her husband that Jesus was a great person. She added, "He taught us to love people for who and what they are—not what you want them to be."

"Charles, do you pray?" I asked next.

"Everyone prays. I pray if there is an emergency. I don't pray for material things. I do pray for people, but I don't pray every day. You don't pray for God to help you grow your tomatoes. You take care of your tomatoes." Charles was doing his famous grin again.

I looked at Ruth who answered, "I don't pray every day. I don't like to be showy about it. All people are different and in how they pray. I pray for my family, friends, and grandkids. I do give thanks."

When I asked Charles if he believed in the Bible, he said, "I don't think it is the word of God but the word of men inspired by God. The Old Testament is a great history lesson."

Ruth added, "I believe the Bible is a great book."

I then asked, "Where do you think you go when you breathe your last breath?"

Charles answered, "When your lights are out, that's it! I would like to think there is eternal life, but it would be awful crowded. In the days when life was hard, and people only lived thirty years or so, eternity was created to help them believe something was better after life."

Ruth finished it with, "That's a hard question. If you haven't been there how would you answer?"

Amazed at how honestly they answered their questions and with this interview completed, we enjoyed another cup of coffee and talked about plans for our next time together.

Walking back to my RV, I remembered a verse from Matthew 22:29 "Love your neighbor as you would love yourself." I looked over my shoulder and waved goodbye to the Williams.

Show No Partiality

Love one another; it's God's greatest command.
He holds each one of us in His mighty hand.
People are different in spirit, heart and mind;
We are God's people and His perfect design.

Friendships take work, and it's not easy labor,
Make an effort to grow close to your neighbor
Be patient when you hear about religion.
Kindness should be our number one ambition.

At the end of our life we won't have to guess.
The mystery of it all will be addressed.
Each one of us has our personal story;
My testimony is to give Christ the glory.

Practical Steps

We are called to love and not exclude anyone because of religious differences.

The Evans

I met Mick and Susan Evans in February, 2007. The following year, I got to know Susan better when we were co-chairwomen for the annual Gulf Shores Women's Club fashion show.

Soon after, I enrolled in classes at the local recreation center and discovered Mick and Susan were taking the same classes. Our gym workouts developed into a genuine friendship and we became fast friends

Occasionally, we would meet for dinner or go to a movie, and we enjoyed each other's company. After we knew each other for a few years, we even took a week trip to the Everglades National Park.

When I called the Evans to ask if I could tell their story, I told them there might be someone they could help if they explained how they dealt with their heartache. Whether it's a loss of a job or a loss of a child, it's comforting to know you're not alone when you experience loss. It is uplifting to witness somebody moving forward even when they didn't feel like it.

The Evans have three children, five grandchildren, and one Umbrella Cockatoo named Casper. Their youngest daughter, Tanya lost her battle with cancer in 1976. She was only five years old.

Tanya got sick while they lived in Saint Louis, Missouri. Some of the best doctors in the world couldn't figure out what was wrong with their little girl. They diagnosed her with pneumonia. Tanya had a favorite stuffed bear she took everywhere and to bed with her at night. However, when it came time to take Tanya to the hospital, she handed her mother the bear and said, "You will need this more than me." Susan thought her daughter knew she would never come back to her home.

Susan told me she still has that bear.

The Evans stayed by their daughter's side during her hospital stay—coloring, reading stories, praying, and hoping things would turn around. Someone had to have an answer.

Susan revealed, "I saw things during Tanya's illness."

"I don't understand. Can you explain this to me?"

"I would dream. See shadows. Hear voices," she replied. "One night I saw, or maybe it was a dream, a cold hand touching me. Then out of nowhere, I heard, 'This is the touch of death.' 'I shot straight up in bed, gasping so hard I woke Mick. He asked me if I was all right. His arms were around me for comfort, and he said, 'Susan! Your arms feel frozen!'"

"One night, I was in the hospital and wanted to pray. I found a chapel down the hall from Tanya's room. When I opened the door, I saw the chapel was empty. I sat down in a pew and began praying. Upon opening my eyes, I saw a white mist and heard a voice say, 'She will be happier with me.'"

"A few days later Tanya asked me, what I was wearing. I realized she couldn't see me. As her health declined, my daughter aged rapidly. The night of her death, she wanted to show me and her dad a photo in a book. Tanya kept saying, "Mom, this picture is beautiful." We looked at all the books in her hospital room and couldn't find the photo Tanya had described. Thoughts swirled in my head that she saw an image of Heaven. After Tanya had closed her eyes for the last time, her skin glowed. She was youthful and beautiful again."

An autopsy was performed. Nine months later, the Evans found out Tanya had a rare form of cancer—only the twentieth case in the world.

After hearing their story, I had one last question to ask,"Where do you think we go after death?"

Mick said, "I don't think there's a hell."

Susan added," I hope I go to Heaven if there's a heaven."

I sighed and said, "Both of you have suffered great despair. Some things are a mystery, but hope is an expectation of something more. If you hope in Heaven, you have to trust the One who created it. Hope gives us a promise of a future. The Bible says, 'Hope does not disappoint,' and three things will last forever—faith, hope, and love. (1Corinthians 13:13)

Most of us have experienced loss in life's storms. We need to mourn our situations, but don't give up on the great Redeemer. Working through the pain is not easy.

Practical Steps

If you can't let go, let God. He will help you embrace hope and grow in it.

Eleanor

Sometimes it takes one little word, a card, or a grasp of the hand. It might mean standing by someone during a particularly hard time and saying nothing at all. I'm sure somebody is struggling just to get through the day right now. When I was attending a meeting of our recipe club, I overheard that a member, Debra Sanders, needed comfort after losing a loved one. Yesterday, my neighbor was in the yard arguing with his son, and I realized that he might be carrying a burden caused by a rebellious child. The Bible is clear that everyone will go through trials and tribulations.

Back in 2000, I didn't understand God's perspective and vision for my life. I was too busy chasing the dollar, but my best memories were moments of encouragement. The Bible says, in Hebrews 3:13 to "encourage one another daily."

One evening, after teaching six hours of gymnastics, I couldn't wait till the class was over. I felt I couldn't lift another kid onto a set of uneven bars. My feet were swollen, and I had pulled a muscle in my back. I waited thirty extra minutes for a parent to pick up her child. When her mother bounded into the gym, she touched my shoulder and said, "I'm sorry I'm late. My daughter is enjoying gymnastics and I'm so glad she has you as a coach. She has improved in her skills and confidence." I never asked her why she was late. It didn't really matter because, in that moment, she encouraged me. That's all it took; I never gave a second thought of how long the day was or how tired I felt.

After moving to Gulf Shores, I wanted to do volunteer work. Bill found an opportunity for me as a consultant at a local pregnancy center. The requirements were tough, but the staff was so gentle and uplifting. Their encouragement kept me going. Because the workers gave me confidence, I finished the training God sent me to do. In return, my whole life changed.

God gives spiritual gifts; one of them is the gift of encouragement. The Bible uses the word *exhortation.* It comes from the Greek word *papakaleo* which means "to exhort" or "to encourage." Exhortation is a key feature of Christianity, but encouragement isn't strictly for Christians; it's for everybody. Great men of the past such as Dwight L. Moody and Billy Sunday had the gift of exhortation. God calls us to take action, but some of us need human motivation. Many people have come into my life not only to encourage me but to help me put God's plans into action.

Eleanor Motta proved to be one of my biggest encouragers. She is 54 years old and was born in Brazil. Eleanor and her family arrived in America in 1985 when she was twenty-five. She was self-taught; she had no formal education but spoke five languages.

I first met Eleanor at the House of Prayer where I was teaching a women's group. After the study was over, I made an announcement that God had been prompting me to write, and I needed help for this undertaking. Eleanor came forward and said she had experience as a freelance writer and would like to assist me. I asked her to tell me about her background. She said, "I owned and was editor/publisher of a newspaper for six years. The paper served subscriptions to eighteen states and twenty-two countries." After chatting for a while, I knew I could learn a lot from her. She had a ministry to serve others with the gifts and talents that God has given her.

Eleanor never charged me for her time. One day I asked her, "Why do you give away advice and wisdom so freely?"

She said, "I heard from the Lord, 'Freely you receive, freely you give.' It's is taken from Matthew 10:8."

Writing is a passion for Eleanor; her favorite quote is from Heidi Baker, "I'm just a little brush in the hands of a mighty God."

Eleanor and her three sons moved from Florida to South Alabama in 1998. Ten years later, she went to a women's religious convention. While there, she accepted Christ. Eleanor said, "I was a people-pleaser, and that is what I thought people wanted me to do, but there was no change in my life."

Afterwards, she and her family began attending an evangelical church. Her pastor asked her to translate a wedding and a baptism. While studying the Word, she asked the Holy Spirit to reveal what the scriptures meant. Eleanor said, "A supernatural thing happened! I really did find Jesus! I had a new understanding and love for God and people." God says in Ezekiel 36:26: "A new heart will I give you, and a new spirit will I put within you."

It is hard to spend time with Eleanor and talk about writing. We'd rather share what God is doing in our lives! It is uplifting to hear her talk about her experiences, family, and faith.

During one of our times together she told me her son Valen was getting married. I asked her, "Will the happy couple need a wedding coordinator?"

Grinning, she said, "I think so. Why?"

"I would like to offer my help as a wedding coordinator to you and your family. Remember, I have coordinated dozens of weddings."

After I had hung up, I thought to myself, *Isn't God smart! In His wisdom, Proverbs 18:24 tells us*, "Friends come and go, but a true friend sticks by you like family."

God took my casual acquaintance with Eleanor to a different level. First, our relationship changed from one with common interests to one in which we are sisters in Christ. Then it changed, and Eleanor became my mentor. I have a need to know someone is there who believes in me. Words refresh our souls and cost nothing, but, an encouraging friend means everything. Eleanor is a girlfriend devoted to putting love into action.

Words that Encourage

Language is a gift that can inspire others;
Words are like bread that feeds the soul.
Recall a time when somebody spoke
A kind remark that echoes in your mind.
Everyone struggles and wants support.
What joy to know, we are not alone.

Encouragement is for everyone,
As we face trials and battles.
The power to inspire a friend
Is sweeter than the taste of wine.
Words of hope are songs to one's ear.
What joy to know, we are not alone.

Encouragers can bring out our best,
Leveling rough places in family and life.
They are builders of visions and dreams,
Cheering us on to the finish line.
Like quenching rain to parched lips,
What joy to know, we are not alone.

Practical Steps

Love from the center of who you are.

Mark

I smile every time I think of Mark. He is a kind, sensitive, educated man and was our tour guide when we traveled to Israel. I was hoping to catch Mark alone during our trip, but it never happened. He did agree to stay in touch after the tour was over. I was thrilled he was open to sharing his Jewish faith; even if it was by email. Most people think twice about sharing personal information with a virtual stranger, and most wouldn't take the time to follow up on a casual request. It's funny to me how we are more worried about what other people think of us than what God thinks of us.

Mark grew up in Montreal and went to a Modern Orthodox school and synagogue. Most of the kids were not religious as he was, and religion was not dominant in their lives. His family stressed secular studies. Over the years, he had tried to fill what he felt was the missing part of his understanding of the world.

After we returned to Alabama, I received a return email from Mark. The subject line said *Not easy*. He wrote with sincerity, and I found honesty and heart in his thoughts. Tears washed my face like fresh rain when I finished reading his email:

God is the great being, master of all. Moral but confusing. So many beautiful things He does, but it hurts seeing all the evil. I turn to him, and believe, but it depresses me to see the bad. Jesus is part of God and the human face of the divine. Does that make him the Messiah? Maybe, but that is something I haven't worked out. Being Jewish, I will not go there because I am happy with my family, people, and land. I talk to God. More so over the years. My work with wonderful Christians has helped me to develop this conversation. Their faith has affected me. I believe in the Bible and its essence. There are many questions about its truth, myth, and symbols. I think they are all the same when it comes to helping men understand and strength to cope with the world. After death, I hope to go to Heaven. What exactly that means, I don't know. I do believe from the Jewish point of view we are capable of making a better world. Heaven is after we have done the most for now.

I treasure Mark's testimony because I'm not sure if I will ever have the opportunity to visit with him in Israel again. One thing of which I am confident is that God's love is unstoppable, and there is not a place or person on earth that His love can't reach.

Practical Steps

Let there be peace on earth and let it begin with me.

Family Connections

Relations can be extremely rewarding and extraordinarily challenging, whether you're the parent or the adult child. My relationships with my family members are some of the most enduring and meaningful roles I play in life. It's taken years to build these relationships. The Lord has given me many blessings over the years, and they started with my family.

Clinton

Tim Parker walked into Dance N Things looking for dance tights. I looked up from my desk and was surprised to see a man in the shop. I asked if I could help. He said, "I need a small pair of tights for my niece. She has a recital soon in Chattanooga."

"You have come to the right place. Please, follow me."

I showed him the different colors, and he said, "I'll take three pairs."

After he had paid for the merchandise, he asked if there were any restaurants nearby.

I said, "There is a Chinese restaurant in the shopping center."

He hesitated a few seconds, tilted his head to the side, and said, "I wondered if you have dinner plans for this evening, and if you like Chinese food."

Gazing at him I murmured, "No, I don't, and yes, I do."

"Great! My name is Tim Parker, and what time do you get finished?"

"My name is Linda, and I can be finished when I want, since I own the store."

He edged closer, "I have a few more errands. Would six o'clock be okay?"

"Sounds like a plan. Come back to the store and we'll walk there."

Tim was easy going, and we hit it off immediately. Six years later, my son Clinton arrived on schedule in an Atlanta hospital on a hot July morning. As soon as he entered this world, Clinton was adored and loved by all. As a young boy, he was happy, content, and had an easy-going personality. Since I owned the dance and gym academy, it was easy to bring him to work with me when I didn't have a sitter. He was content staying in his playpen while the secretary kept an eye on him.

Clinton grew into a youngster at the studio. He was a patient little fellow, waiting for me to take care of business and close up shop. I remember one particular evening when Clinton was about seven years old. After six hours of teaching, we were leaving the studio, and I had his thin hand in mine, and I was carrying clothes for both of us, the money bag, and the accounts receivable book. As I was trying to close and lock the door, I dropped everything, and Clinton fell backwards.

I reached for him to see if he was hurt and, being tired and stressed, I wanted to cry.

My voiced cracked as I picked him up and asked, "Are you okay, Son?"

He replied, "I'm okay, Mommy. You're tired. You have worked hard all day. Let me help you pick up your stuff."

My heart ached to see this child so unselfish and so giving to think of me instead of himself. We finally made it home and grabbed something to eat, and I tucked him and myself into bed.

The next day, when I got home from work, I found a written page in his book bag. The page was titled *The Things I Love about My Mother*. Clinton had written, "I love my mom, but wish she didn't work such long hours. All I want is to spend more time with her."

For the next five years I frequently thought about what my son had written, but truthfully, I didn't know how to change my circumstances, or maybe I didn't want to.

Unfortunately, my relationship with Tim didn't work out, and we went our separate ways. Tim was faithful giving his time to Clinton but not so much with the financial responsibilities. I worked more hours to compensate and to save for the future. Therefore, I missed a lot of quality time with Clinton on the weekends. It was easier for Tim to take care of Clinton, and for me to make extra money.

Clinton lived full time with me until he turned twelve. I knew retirement and a move to Alabama were in my near future, so I sought counsel from his teachers on the best way to make the transition.

Clinton always enjoyed his weekends with his dad, but those times were 'fun-and-games' weekends, not like everyday life. The advice from the teachers was to allow Clinton to live with Tim full time to see what it was like when he had to do his homework, brush his teeth, clean up after himself, and do chores.

I talked it over with Tim, and he agreed that Clinton should stay with him. Because Tim lived in another state, I gave him power of attorney to make decisions at school functions, not realizing everything that implied. I was glad Clinton's life in Tennessee was not disrupted, as it took months for me to sell properties, inventory, and furnishings of thirty-two years in business and to move to my new home in Gulf Shores.

One day after I completed the move, I picked up Clinton drove him to Alabama. Showing him his bedroom I said, "This is your new home." I thought he would have a better life living with me and it was time for him to come home.

Clinton was shocked and not happy how I made the decision about his new move without talking it over with him and his father. He was reluctant but started school in Gulf Shores. Three months later, a Tennessee judge decided Tim should have custody of our thirteen-year old son. I had lost my parental rights by moving out of state. I fought the court's decisions, but I couldn't get what I wanted most—my son. Every day I hated myself for being so stupid and blind. Clinton's feelings toward me were strained. Every two weeks, I made my child support payments, but I'm not sure he was ever told that I sent the money or received my cards and letters. Tim refused to communicate, and when we did talk occasionally, there were many accusations. Our relationship as parents was tense for many years, so I buried myself in volunteer work and tried to put my energy into finding my way back to God.

As a teenager, Clinton enjoyed music, writing rap songs, and working hard to perfect his art. He had high hopes his passion would turn to a successful career. I supported his dreams.

Achieving high grades in high school was not a priority, though. Therefore, after graduating from high school and attending a few semesters of college, Clinton felt he was wasting his time. He gave up college and began working as a server in a local steak house. While working, he was living with his father, saving his money. After a few months of collecting a paycheck, he called to say, "Mom, I saved enough money to put a down payment on a truck. I'm happy with my life." After hanging up the phone I thought, *He's content and is going to be ok.*

My son was turning into a responsible man, and I was proud of him. It seemed like yesterday he was asking for crayons and coloring books, and now he owned a truck! Clinton continued with his music, went to work faithfully, and made his truck payments on time. The restaurant demanded he work long hours, but after three years, he saw no advancement and began looking for other employment. A local family-owned restaurant had an opening, and the hours were better. He applied for the job and got it, along with more money and Sundays off.

When Clinton turned twenty, we began spending quality time getting to know each other again. I think he was beginning to understand that I had made choices in life the best way I knew how. He would say, "Mom, you have always been a strong, independent woman, but you've changed! You're finally putting family first in your life."

Clinton and his buddy came to spend his twenty-first birthday in Gulf Shores. We had so much fun that we decided to spend every birthday of his together. Birthdays turned into most holidays. He burns up the highway to be with me now.

For several years, I had shared with Clinton how close my relationship with the Lord had become. My son was very private with his thoughts and comments about religion. He told me often it wasn't cool to talk about church and God with his peers. In April, 2015, I called Clinton to let him know I was in town for the Easter weekend. There was excitement in his voice as he gushed, "Something wonderful has happened to me. I will tell you tomorrow morning when we get together."

I was anxious to hear about this unexpected enthusiasm in his life!

The next day I sat in my car waiting and felt this was an important turn in our relationship. After he got out of his truck, I said, "Hi! Get in the car. Don't keep me in suspense. Please, tell me what has happened to you?!"

Clinton's very words were, "I found Jesus." My heart burst with joy. What a great comfort to a Christian mother to hear those three words.

"Give me all the details," I said, holding back tears.

He told me there was a middle-aged man named Tony who worked with him at the restaurant. Tony was a good friend—a Christian who showed the love of Jesus like no other person he knew. Clinton kept asking Tony to listen to his rap music. Finally, Tony gave in. After listening to a few songs

Tony said, "You have an excellent talent. Do you know your talents come from God?"

What a defining moment for my son! It changed his destiny. Clinton left work that evening with conviction in his heart. The love and kindness of one man helped Clinton rethink the direction for his music, his relationships with others, and his Creator. He realized he was not glorifying God with his music; because his verses had a lot of dark thoughts and profanity. He felt regret for his past actions and had a desire to please God with his future actions. Since then, Clinton boldly proclaims Jesus as his personal Savior! His faith in Jesus is personal, but not selfish. Clinton is not ashamed to tell his experience with Jesus. Today, He uses his gift of music to write Christian songs that praise the Lord. I am thankful for the guidance of Christian people like Tony that make an impact on the younger generation.

Over the years, the relationship I have with Clinton has changed. I have his respect, and we have a common purpose in writing. I imagine if God reconciled His relationship with His children on Earth through Jesus, he would also make a way for mothers and fathers to restore their relationships with their children.

Clinton and I talk about the past, but we don't stay there. Instead, Clinton and I focus celebrating life together in the present and imagining the possibilities of the future.

Practical Steps

Dance and sing your way through every single day.

Claire

My Mother, Claire Marie Goerig, was born at home in Philadelphia, Pennsylvania in 1927. Her only sibling, Carolyn, was born five years later. Their grandfather, Pop, took both of them to Catholic mass every Sunday. As a girl, she felt different from her Protestant friends and remembers them making fun of the ashes of a cross on her forehead each Ash Wednesday.

On a blind date, when she was seventeen, Claire met Henry Joe Ray, Jr., from Monterey, Tennessee. He was stationed at the Philadelphia naval base while his submarine, the USS Devilfish, was commissioned. After two weeks of dating, they eloped. When Claire told her parents, her dad was ashamed and moved out of the house. The newlyweds moved in. Her father eventually came home, and her husband of three months went off to war. They were separated for thirteen months while he served in Europe.

Upon Henry's return from World War II, he began studying at Tennessee Tech in Cookeville, Tennessee, and Claire gave birth to a son. Shortly after Henry graduated with a degree in electrical engineering, the news of another baby surprised both my parents. That surprise was me.

Between moves, my sister Andrea was born. When Andrea was nine after my parents had been married twenty-five years, my father's restlessness got the best of him and he asked my mother for a divorce. Three years later, they remarried and lived in Dalton, Georgia, only to have Dad die of a heart attack at the age of 51, six months later.

Mother and Andrea continued to live in the same apartment where Dad died. Unfortunately, Dad had not made provisions for his family, so when Andrea was 12, Mother began working outside the home. She found an office job at Alden Industries in Calhoun, Georgia, and was in the workforce for the first time in her life at age 47. She felt like a bird out of a cage. She had gone from being a teenager under her father's rules, to a married woman tied down with children and a controlling husband, and now, at last, to being a breadwinner.

One night, a few friends from Alden decided to kick up their heels and meet at the Holiday Inn for drinks and music. There, Mother met Doug Horn. An hour or so went by, and the Alden gang left the bar to hang out at Doug's apartment. Mother later said, "I knew Doug was interested because he couldn't keep his eyes or hands off me." A few days later, Doug called Mother and asked her out. After several dates, she wondered why Doug was never around on weekends. He told her he went to Atlanta to visit his family. My mother was hurt and shocked when, six months later, she found out that 'family' included a wife.

Doug was a successful businessman and had a lot of money and knew how to entice Mom to stay with him. Mother had never had the opportunity to experience male relationships other than the one with Henry, so she made the decision to keep things like they were and was satisfied to see Doug when she could.

Two years later, Mother was sitting with a neighbor, Louise, at the pool in their apartment complex. Louise told mom a young pastor and his wife had moved into town. They started a church in a storefront and named it Holy Baptist Church. Louise and Mom decided to attend a service, and, afterward, the pastor came to visit Mother. Since nobody was home, Pastor Johnson left a tract under her door.

In the months that followed, Mother dealt with surviving as a single parent coping with her sister's cancer diagnosis, and needing comfort and strength for herself. Alone in her apartment one day, she remembered the tract left by Pastor Johnson. She rummaged through drawers until she found it, and she began to read each word with the pages becoming wet from the tears rolling down her cheeks. The cover of the little pamphlet showed one person talking to another with the words, "I've got Good News. (John 3:16) For God so loved the world that He gave His only begotten son, that whosoever believeth in Him should not perish, but have everlasting life."

The booklet began, "What stands in your way of receiving this free gift, right now?" Her eyes glanced at the next page. "There is one problem. Sin! (Romans 3:23) All have sinned." Slowly, she turned the page. "Christ died on the Cross, was buried and arose. (Romans 5:8) While we were sinners, Christ died for us."

Mother's eyes started to burn, and her hand shook as she moved to read the next page. "Just believe, confess, repent, and commit! (Romans 10:9) If you confess with your mouth Jesus is Lord, and believe in your heart that God raised Him from the dead, you shall be saved." She turned to the last page and read, "It only takes a simple act of faith to trust Jesus and give Him control of your life." She closed the track and saw a question on the back page. "Are you willing to trust and receive Jesus right now as your Savior?"

After Mother read the last question, she fell to her knees and surrendered her life to Christ. She doesn't remember how long she was on the floor praying and weeping, but when she stood up, she felt the presence of God and a sense of new peace.

The next morning, she reached for the telephone and heard Doug's voice say, "Hello, Claire."

Mother's voiced cracked with remorse as she told Doug it was over and that she was now a Christian, and Christians don't date married men. Doug laughed and said, "Call me when your God doesn't fill your needs anymore."

For the next ten years, Mother attended Holy Baptist before visiting a Pentecostal event called the Holy Ghost Rally. There, she received the gift of tongues, and a guest evangelist prophesied she was a gifted prayer warrior. Since receiving this gift, she has spent forty years as a prayer warrior, praying for people with problems or burdens.

My mother is the first person I call if I have a prayer request. One day recently, it was important for me to hear her views on life after death. She answered my questions leaning close to me with her laugh lines growing deeper. "If the rapture doesn't come first, I will go to Heaven. I pray that when I face my Maker, I don't stand ashamed. I made mistakes."

"Mother, we all have made mistakes, sinned, and fallen short. Where is that in scripture?" I asked, scrunching my forehead together.

Mother smiled and replied, "Romans 3:23."

Then I asked her what she is most proud of, and she replied easily, "All my children are saved, in church, and they serve the Lord."

Young in heart, my mother's body grows older each day, but her love for the Lord is her legacy to her children, grandchildren, and great-grandchildren. God has prepared a place in His home of Glory, because the Bible tells us when we depart from this life, we are with Christ. To me, that means our Heavenly Father will meet Mother with outstretched arms, and I will reunite with her.

Mother

This poem is to let you know your child is blessed,
When God created mothers, He gave me the best.
Many jewels reflect your faithfulness in your crown,
You taught valuable lessons that will be passed down.

Happily, you sacrificed for us through the years,
Your never ending courage taught us not to fear.
During my worst days, you never left me alone,
I'm grateful that you were my mother in our home.

Practical Steps

Each Christian has a testimony of what God has done in his or her life.

LINDA RAY CENTER

The Grand Finale

There is no perfect relationship here on Earth, but we can find ways to improve how we love. Love is a commandment. Sometimes I struggle with people who are hard to love. So, first, I love God. Mark 12:30 tells me, "Love the Lord your God with all your heart, soul, mind, and strength." That makes things easier. The next verse is equally important: "Love your neighbor as yourself." There are no commandments greater than these.

It's important to share insights connecting Christians, unbelievers, and relationships in general. When it comes to words like *Lord*, *God*, and *trust* we get uncomfortable, and afraid to talk in a civil way.

Let's find a way to live contently in the present relationships that God has given us and communicate without forcing an opinion on others. If anything, each of us needs to give extra attention to people unlike ourselves. Only then, will you and I be loved in return for who we are and what we believe. Embracing the differences is our only good option.

I was amazed with the interaction between my friends that grew from interviewing them for the purpose of this book. I love how they opened up and shared their opinions and life stories. I care for them, but more than that, I know God cares for them. The Bible tells us in Genesis 1:27: *He created humans in His image*. That tells me we are the heart of His affection.

My prayer for you is that before the embers of relationships grow cold because of indifference, may a fresh wind rekindle the flames of love.